Let My People Grow

Let My People Grow

Making disciples who make a difference in today's world

Edited by
Mark Greene and Tracy Cotterell

Authentic

LONDON • ATLANTA • HYDERABAD

licc
The London Institute for Contemporary Christianity

12 11 10 09 08 07 06 7 6 5 4 3 2 1

First published in 2006 by Authentic Media
9 Holdom Avenue, Bletchley, Milton Keynes, MK1 1QR, UK
285 Lynnwood Avenue, Tyrone, GA 30290, USA
OM Authentic Media
Medchal Road, Jeedimetla Village, Secunderabad 500 055, AP, India
www.authenticmedia.co.uk
Authentic Media is a division of Send the Light Ltd., a company limited by guarantee (registered charity no. 270162)

British Library Cataloguing in Publication Data
A catalogue record for this book is available from the British Library

ISBN-13: 978-1-85078-671-9
ISBN-10: 1-85078-671-2

Cover Design by Sam Redwood
Typeset by Temple Design
Print Management by Adare Carwin
Printed and Bound in the UK by J.H. Haynes & Co., Sparkford

Contents

Acknowledgements

We're grateful for the practical help, astute insights and financial support we've received from many quarters in developing this collection. In particular, our thanks go to Muriel Loydell, Tara Smith and Mike Hollow for their contributions to the editorial process; to Charlotte Hubback at Authentic; to 'Friends of LICC'. We deeply appreciate the generosity of all our contributing authors in carving out the time to write, and for their openness in sharing their questions, experience and wisdom.

Tracy Cotterell, Director, Imagine Project
Mark Greene, Executive Director
The London Institute for Contemporary Christianity
October 2006

Tracy Cotterell

After many years in marketing and advertising, Tracy spent three years studying theology at London School of Theology. As Director of LICC's Imagine Project, Tracy is engaged in blending biblical perspectives with practical church-based experimentation to help churches become communities of growing 'whole-life' followers of Christ, better equipped to make a difference in our challenging contemporary UK culture.

Mark Greene

Mark's experience as a young Christian in advertising and as a member of a disciple-making church was hugely significant for his subsequent concern to see other Christians equipped and supported for 'whole-life' discipleship and mission. Now the Director of LICC, he was formerly vice-principal at London School of Theology, where he also studied theology. His essay 'Imagine how we can reach the UK' was a catalyst for the consultation that generated this collection of essays.

Foundations

1

Let my people grow

Mark Greene

What are the driving forces that are increasingly focusing the UK church on this key issue of contemporary disciple-making? Why is *whole-life* disciple-making so crucial for mission in the twenty-first-century UK? How do we approach this challenge of helping people to grow and live integrated, transformative lives of faith wherever they are? In starting to address these questions Mark sets the context for this collection of essays.

For reflection

- To what extent would you describe your church as a disciple-making church?
- In what ways do you think the sacred-secular divide affects you?

Let my people grow

Here's a mystery. In the UK, 4.5 million people go to church once a month or more. Yes, it's fewer than in 1990, fewer than in 1980, and fewer than in 1970. But it is still a lot of people. In fact, it's 4,499,988 more than Jesus started with. On average, each of those people knows at least one hundred other people and talks to, meets with, writes to, calls, emails, texts at least fifty people a week who don't yet know Jesus. They certainly do if they're a 6-year-old in a primary school, a 21-year-old in a college, a 35-year-old in a job, a parent trundling up to the school gate, or a retiree in a home. We have the people to reach our nation.

So why do we seem to be having so little impact? Is it because we don't have PowerPoint in every nave, cappuccinos in every church hall and a Bill Hybels in every pulpit? Is it because actually the Gospel of the crucified and risen Lord hasn't got very much to say to twenty-first-century westerners? That it's neither relevant to the issues we face today nor radical enough to address them?

Well, it's certainly the case that in our rapidly changing post-Christian society it's not easy to know how to respond as a Christian. However, for a growing number of Christians and the writers of this book, one of the primary reasons for our decline is not that society has changed – though it has – but that on the whole in today's church we don't make disciples, we make converts. We don't make apprentices of Jesus, people who are moving forward in their ability to live the life of Christ in every aspect of their lives and to show and share that life wherever God has placed them. Furthermore, a disciple is not just someone with a concern for personal holiness and integrity or for evangelism; he or she has a desire for all that is on the

Lord of all's agenda. Disciples, then, are called to be yeast, agents of transformation seeking to see Christ's kingdom come in every aspect of human culture – intellectual and emotional, economic and artistic, political and domestic, local and global, private and public.

Somehow, however, we have lost sight of the comprehensive implications of Jesus' praxis and his final instructions: 'Go therefore and make disciples of all nations' (Mt. 28:19).

Jesus made disciples. He had a 'train and release' strategy; whilst overall in the UK church we have a 'convert and retain' strategy. As Paul Bayes, National Mission and Evangelism Advisor to the Church of England, put it, 'I can show you praying churches and preaching churches and social action churches and teaching churches, but I can think of very few disciple-making churches.'

Similarly, whilst Jesus invested a huge amount of time in training a small number of apprentices, very few of our church leaders are actively engaged in a similar kind of intentional, relational disciple-making. Why is it, we might ask, that our best-trained pastors and teachers spend so little time doing what Jesus spent so much of his time doing?

In his chapter in this collection, Martyn Atkins reminds us of David Watson's passionate assertion, '*Discipleship* sums up Christ's plan for the world.'[1] He goes on to write

> Discipleship . . . for all its brilliant simplicity . . . is the one approach that most western churches have neglected. Instead we have reports, commissions, conferences, seminars, missions, crusades, reunion schemes, liturgical reforms – the lot. But very little attention has been given to discipleship.[2]

Now discipleship and disciple-making are not optional extras in the Christian life, like chocolate biscuits at a church meeting. Disciple-making is a scriptural imperative, a pastoral imperative and a missional imperative.

Disciple-making is a scriptural imperative because Jesus told us to do it. It is a pastoral imperative because in a rapidly changing, often bewildering, high-paced culture people need to know how to live the Christian life consistently. It is a missional imperative because people in our culture are not looking simply for a truth to assent to, but for a way to live an authentic, adventurous, meaningful life where they are.

Importantly, the pastoral imperative is directly linked to the missional imperative. After all, if the Gospel does not make any difference to the way I live my 'ordinary' life – to my desires and priorities, or to my stressful job or my fractious marriage – what kind of Gospel do I have to share with my friends and colleagues, whose major issues may well also be their stressful jobs or their unfulfilling relationships? Is Christianity merely a leisure-time option – a Sunday service to attend, a home group to come along to? No, the Gospel is not just a way into a relationship with Christ in eternity, it is a way into abundant life now – in sickness as well as in health, in limitation as well as in opportunity, in the kitchen as well as the sanctuary, in the board as well as the sitting room.

If we are to confidently share the Gospel in our culture, we not only need to be sure that it is true but also convinced that 'it works'. We need a testimony to the difference Christ makes to our lives. Indeed, unless we are learning and growing in our ability to live as followers of Christ in our society, we may testify to the eternal significance of the death that Christ died but we will have no testimony to the life that he offers now.

Effective evangelism cannot be separated from dynamic discipleship. Indeed, in a consumer culture where what works can be more important than what is true, the life-transforming power of the Gospel is vital in persuading some people to consider its truth.

The sacred-secular divide

A major reason for this failure to equip followers of Christ for all of life is the impact of the sacred-secular divide on Christians and their church communities. The sacred-secular divide is the pervasive belief that some things are important to God – church, prayer meetings, social action, Alpha, Christianity Explored – but that other human activities are at best neutral: work, school, college, sport, the arts, leisure, rest, sleep. This view has had a devastating impact on two key areas of Christian life – our mission and our living. This was confirmed by the broad-scale questionnaire research that followed the publication of *Imagine how we can reach the UK*.[3] The vast majority of Christians have not been helped to see that who they are and what they do every day in schools, workplaces or clubs is significant to God, nor to understand that the people they spend time with in those everyday contexts are the people God is calling them to pray for, bless and witness to. Similarly, in the nine consultations we held in partnership with the Evangelical Alliance with leaders representing some 300,000 Christians, these leaders confirmed that this was one of the major challenges they faced and one of the greatest opportunities to be grasped.

Overall, people in the church have increasingly seen themselves as marginalised, in a corner, up against the ropes. The reality, however, is that the people of God are not skulking in a corner. From Monday to Monday the people of God are in the world – in schools, colleges, workplaces, clubs. The people of God are out there relating to scores of people every week. But we have simply not been envisioned, resourced and supported to share the good news of Jesus in our everyday contexts. Every Christian is a missionary, every Christian is a minister, every Christian is a full-time Christian worker – an FTCW.

Just imagine what would happen if church communities started to pray by name for the people that their members spent their Monday to Friday lives with? And just imagine too what would happen if church communities really grasped the comprehensive scope of the salvation that Jesus came to bring, and began to affirm and support church members in their desires to see God's 'kingdom come' in local government, in the arts, in transport, amongst the poor and elderly, in concern for the environment. Concerns for mission and emissions are not mutually exclusive. On the contrary. Jesus, after all, is not just the co-creator of 'all things', as Colossians 1 reminds us, but he is the one through whom 'all things, whether things on earth or things in heaven' are reconciled.

Let my people grow

In sum, there is a widely researched, clearly expressed need to create church communities that intentionally, graciously and humbly seek to help God's people grow. And as can be seen from the wide range of churchmanship represented in the contributors to this collection, this isn't limited to one particular denomination or to churches with one particular emphasis, whether charismatic or reformed.

The challenge to the contemporary church, therefore, is not only how to fulfil our mission to 'the lost' but also how to help 'the found' to grow. The success of the one is dependent on the other. You cannot do mission without maturing in the process. And you cannot mature in Christ without being involved in God's mission to transform people and culture.

However, there is no point in flagellating ourselves about what we haven't done or what we don't know: what we need is a church culture that is realistic about where we are but also ambitious about where we might end up. As Paul put it,

> We proclaim him, admonishing and teaching everyone with all wisdom, so that we may present everyone perfect in Christ. To this end I labour, struggling with all his energy, which so powerfully works in me (Col. 1:28-29, NIV).

Paul wants people not just to know Christ but to be 'perfect in Christ'. He wants them to grow. Not just for their own sake, as a kind of self-focused, self-indulgent exercise in self-improvement. No, the biblical concern for growth in discipleship is rooted in mission, as David Firth points out in his essay on Old Testament disciple-making.[4] Growth in discipleship is vital to fulfilling the mission God has called us to.

Of course, the challenge to submit all of our life to Christ is a daunting one – Jesus said many hard things to his disciples. How much more comfortable it is to limit Christ's real involvement to my church activities. How hard and even frightening it can be to open up all of my life to Christ. What might that mean for my job? For my relationships with friends or family? But, excitingly, we may learn as much or more about who God really is through our experiences of him outside the church as we do from our lives inside it. The church should be a place that intentionally opens our eyes to see and seek God in those contexts.

Changing the default setting

This is a challenge for individuals and also for church leaders. How do we change the default setting of our communities so that they do become places where our relationships, our conversations, the stories we tell and the heroes we praise are suffused with the desire to help one another fulfil our God-given calling wherever we are, at whatever stage of life?

In the last five years or so, there have been many encouraging experiments and much helpful reflection on new forms of church. But the key issue is not the *form* that a church takes but whether the goal of the community is to make whole-life disciples. After all, our task is not just to get people into a traditional parish church, or a café-church or a pub discussion, or a post-clubbing chill-out or a stadium gig. Our commission is not just to get people converted and then, as Jason Clark put it, 'warehouse them for heaven', as if the only wondrous gift Jesus came to lavish on his followers was life after death. Rather, we're here to help one another explore the high and mysterious adventure of living the whole life of Christ in a fallen world. We're here to help one another become fully engaged *now* in living, applying and sharing the difference Jesus makes wherever he has placed us.

Sadly, for many Christians, the very word 'disciple' conjures up a negative picture of programmes and systems, of getting bogged down in acquiring information about Christianity but losing the whoosh and whoompf of the daily adventure of walking with Christ. But true disciple-making is about liberating people to become more fully human, even as we become more like Christ.

Plotting a pathway through this collection

As you read on into the chapters that follow you'll see that from a variety of perspectives, each contributor soberly but hopefully explores major discipleship challenges facing the body of Christ. Many of them directly or indirectly wrestle with issues facing leaders who seek to create a disciple-making context in their local church. So in this collection there are lessons from Scripture, lessons from the experience of Christians in the early church and lessons from the eighteenth century. There are lessons, too, from pastors trying to work through the implications of the call to whole-life, whole-loaf discipleship in the context of different local churches today – in the Baptist and Anglican traditions, in cells and within the emerging church. And there are insights from experts in other disciplines seeking to come alongside churches to help them make such changes.

Still, for all the enthusiasm for the task and involvement of the contributors, this is not a collection that seeks to provide or point to some new programme or new resource, or to some off-the-shelf, all-dancing, all-singing, change-the-church-by-Tuesday-win-the-world-by-Thursday solution. Indeed, as Phil Meadows writes in his chapter on Wesley,

> Wesley calls into question our desire for off-the-shelf solutions to ministry needs, especially those technological approaches to church leadership and

> disciple-making that make gurus out of 'successful' pastors. Often concealed behind the visible success of churches we admire are stories of modest beginnings and endurance through real struggles to pursue a vision of authentic Christian discipleship.[5]

All the contributors point to resources that may well help. Yet there is an exhilarating humility zinging through this material – we don't have all the answers, we're thinking this through; we're trying to move forward. Still, that doesn't mean that there isn't food for the journey here or that the writers in this collection, or we at LICC, are content to meander merrily along. On the contrary, at LICC we have initiated an experimental pilot scheme which will work with twelve or so churches over a three-year period to explore how indeed we can begin to create church communities that have whole-life apprentice-making at the heart of their values. Similarly, you'll hear of other experiments in the wider UK church that are seeking to bring biblical faith to bear on making fruitful, maturing human disciples in today's world.

Here, then, is a collection of biblical, theological and practical reflections that aims to unpack the challenges, to focus our vision, to stimulate the imagination and point to some signposts for the work that we need to do as the body of Christ. For all the diversity of background and roles of the contributors, some common themes emerge:

- The need in any age, in any culture to find a theology that works
- The reality that life and faith and mission are integrated and need to stay that way
- The need to clarify a vision for whole-life discipleship and what we understand a growing disciple of Christ to look like today

- The need for intentionality
- The need to develop leadership teams, not just pastor-heroes, equipped to tackle these challenges

The apprentice-making church is not an elite training centre headed up by a world-class scholar, it's a place where *all* who are involved help each other to move along the path towards maturity in Christ. It's not just for adults, it's for children and teenagers too. Indeed, it's vital, as Jason Gardner argues, for young people to see adults intentionally seeking to grow.[6] And it's vital for young people to be discipled by adults, particularly by their parents.

The collection is thus intended to offer some signposts for the journey ahead, and we hope you'll want to contribute to the directions by posting your own comments, suggestions and insights on the *Imagine* section of LICC's website – www.licc.org.uk/imagine/comments. You might also want to involve others in responding to the issues by using the questions at the beginning of the chapters as stimuli or by photocopying a particularly intriguing chapter and discussing it in a home group or team meeting.

Personally, I've found new insights and wisdom in every chapter of this collection. My prayer, and that of my fellow editor, is that it will deepen your personal commitment to being an apprentice of Christ in every aspect of your life, that it will strengthen your commitment to support others in their apprenticeship, and that it will inspire you to work towards creating church communities that intentionally and proactively seek to fulfil Christ's focus on mission and maturity, to the glory of God and the fruitfulness of his mission in our land and beyond.

♦ ♦ ♦ ♦

Further reading and resources

See this book's Postcript, 'Creating disciple-making churches today: The *Imagine Project*' for a range of resources including the essay *Imagine how we can reach the UK*

Rabey, Steve and Lois (eds.), *Side by Side, A Handbook – Disciple-making for a New Century* (Cook Communications Ministries, 2000)

Willard, Dallas, *The Divine Conspiracy: Rediscovering our Hidden Life in God* (Fount, 1998)

Notes

1 David Watson, *Discipleship* (Hodder & Stoughton, 1981).
2 See chapter 4: From darkness to light.
3 See www.licc.org.uk/imagine/research for the published survey.
4 See chapter 2: What did Moses do? Discipleship BC.
5 See chapter 5: The 'end' of discipleship.
6 See chapter 12: As a young person, what would Jesus do?

Reflections on Scripture

2

What did Moses do? Discipleship BC

David Firth

David has experience in pastoral and evangelistic ministry in his native Australia, as well as seven years' service with the Australian Baptist Missionary Society in Zimbabwe and South Africa. He is presently Old Testament Tutor at Cliff College in Derbyshire. His research interests are in Old Testament ethics and mission, with a particular focus on literary issues associated with narrative and poetry.

In this chapter David opens up the Old Testament to provide a context in which discipleship in the New Testament can be more meaningfully understood. He argues that discipleship can never be the goal itself. It is only meaningful when seen within the framework of God's mission. Old Testament leaders are called by God to help his people live out his mission among the nations. This provides a pattern both for New Testament discipleship and for us today.

For reflection

- What is your understanding of God's mission in the world today?
- How does it impact your own discipleship and the disciple-making in your church?

What did Moses do? Discipleship BC

When Jesus first called the twelve, the gospel accounts present them as responding immediately, with no obvious uncertainty as to the type of role to which they were being called.[1] Very clearly, even though Jesus was going to be a leader like no other, they already had a sense of what it meant to be a disciple. The concept was not something that Jesus introduced, even though he did give it a radical twist. Conceptually, therefore, discipleship must be something that reaches back into Jewish identity, something that was well established long before Jesus.

Yet something curious happens when one picks up popular books on discipleship. Most of these will have something to say on the biblical foundation of discipleship. Or at least, it will be called biblical. But if we examine these in detail, something becomes particularly clear: for 'biblical' we should read 'New Testament'. There is absolutely nothing wrong with looking at the New Testament for what it teaches us on discipleship. After all, it is the place where we read about Jesus and his work with the twelve, along with the other disciples that we find peopling its pages. As Christians, we cannot understand discipleship unless we understand what the New Testament has to say, and what the New Testament says is clearly biblical.

But there is something wrong with either our terminology or our theology if all we have is the New Testament's perspective on this crucial concept. A biblical theology of discipleship needs to encompass the message of the whole Bible, and that means examining the witness of the Old Testament as well. In short, if we are going to understand why the concept of discipleship was already established at the time of Jesus and the twelve, we need to understand the framework for discipleship already present in the Old Testament.[2]

That said, we should note that there is not an obvious surplus of texts in the Old Testament that overtly deal with the theme of discipleship, though throughout these Scriptures we read the exhortation to the older generation to pass on wisdom to the next. In some translations, the word disciple will not occur. Even its most likely occurrence, in Isaiah 8:16, does not offer too much, beyond suggesting that Isaiah had some disciples who followed him in his prophetic ministry and who were in some way taught by him. Indeed, the word often translated here as 'disciples' occurs in only five other places,[3] always with reference to some form of instruction, but not normally with the specific sense of discipleship. But in any case, looking for certain words is not really the way to go, because discipleship can be enacted and embodied without key words being used.

Discipleship in the Old Testament is about following those called by God to provide leadership for his people. But it has a specific purpose, namely to live out the mission of God among his people as they in turn witness to God as the one who dwells among them. Discipleship can never, therefore, simply be a goal in and of itself. Discipleship is only meaningful when it is seen within the framework of God's mission.[4] When we understand it in those terms, there are significant parts of the Old Testament that shed light on Jesus' own practices in discipling the twelve. Two sets of texts are particularly important: Moses and his training of Joshua, and the account of Elijah and Elisha. What will become evident through these texts is that Moses functions as a model disciple-maker, and that discipleship always points beyond itself to God's wider mission. Discipleship in the Old Testament can thus be shaped by the question 'What did Moses do?' That this continues to be important in the New Testament is immediately apparent when we note the ways in which all four gospel writers portray Jesus in the light of Moses. Thus, the Old Testament provides a context in which discipleship in the New Testament can be more meaningfully understood.

Moses and Joshua

One of the perennial problems of leadership for Moses was the need to share responsibility around. There are two accounts in the Pentateuch of times when he was encouraged to bring others into a leadership role, subsidiary to himself, in order to enable all the work of the community to continue in a practical and effective manner.[5] Both of these accounts are largely concerned with administrative matters, such as the hearing of minor grievances and the arrangements for the distribution of food. But even before the first of these, we encounter Joshua[6] as an important leader, commanding the Israelite army engaged with Amalek.[7] Although the exact chronology of events in Exodus 15:22-18:27 can be difficult to determine, it is clear that Joshua had already come to prominence. At this point, we see him primarily as a military leader, albeit one whose victory was achieved more by virtue of Moses being able to keep his staff in the air than through his own military genius.

It quickly becomes clear that Joshua's role in relation to Moses is not purely military, as the rest of the Pentateuch shows him in a variety of roles, all of them involved with providing support to Moses. This is apparent from the time we encounter Joshua in Exodus 24:13, where he is described as Moses' 'assistant'.[8] The narrative makes clear that Joshua is one of seventy Israelite elders who go up onto Mount Sinai in order to ratify the covenant agreement with God that has been outlined in chapters 20-23. Aaron and Hur, who were in the battle against Amalek, are also present, but they take on a less significant role than Joshua. What distinguishes Joshua is that he is presented as the one who is determined to enable Moses to complete his role, even though we are never told why this might be. Indeed, he even acts as the one to initially advise Moses of problems back in the camp,[9] though like the disciples in the gospels he is quite capable of completely missing the point. Joshua retains his commitment to the work of Moses, as is particularly obvious in the account of the tent of meeting,[10] where he remained so that Moses could return to the main camp.

Joshua is not mentioned at all in Leviticus, but he is prominent in the book of Numbers. In this book's account of Moses sharing out his workload, Joshua is once again among the seventy elders and has to be mildly rebuked by Moses for failing to discern that the work of God's Spirit should not be restricted to an elite.[11] But he takes on a more important role as one of the spies exploring the land. He and Caleb are the only ones to recognise the reality of Yahweh's gift, and are accordingly promised that they alone of their generation will enter the land of promise.[12] In this he begins to demonstrate a pattern of leadership, even if it is not widely acknowledged. The presence of the Spirit in his life was something that God recognised when he directed Moses to appoint him as his successor.[13] Moses had, in fact, prayed that God would replace him with someone who would act as a wise shepherd for the nation, and Joshua was the answer to that prayer. Moreover, Joshua was one of those who would be responsible for the division of the land.[14] The one who had worked and journeyed with Moses, who had been trained by him, was the one whom God called to lead his people into the land of promise.

We cannot know what initially brought Joshua to prominence, nor is there any evidence of Moses intentionally taking him on as a disciple, though the fact that he is called Moses' assistant would at least suggest there was a relationship that moved in that direction. What is striking is that his life and personal formation equipped him for the role to which God called him, and that he carried out that role in a way that looked back to Moses. In part, of course, events happened because God led Joshua along a certain path, but there is no denying that his own approach to leading the people of God was modelled on that of Moses. Thus, when the opportunity arose to enter the land, he followed Moses' pattern of first sending in spies.[15] Anyone reading the account of the crossing of the Jordan cannot miss the clear allusions to the crossing of the Red Sea.[16] As with Moses, the celebration of Passover was a vital first step in public ministry,[17] whilst Joshua also encountered God in a special way when he was told to remove his sandals because he was standing on holy ground.[18] One could say God was at work, showing through these parallels that Joshua was indeed a leader who was called to follow Moses. But at each point, Joshua also modelled his actions on those of Moses. Although the term may be anachronistic at this point, discipleship was clearly an important issue for Joshua. As he sought to work out the implications of his own call to ministry and leadership, he saw the need to do so within the framework established by Moses. The implications of his training could only be discerned once his own call was understood, but it was in the context of his own ministry that his discipleship could really be worked out.

Elijah and Elisha

We cannot take time here to examine all the stories about Elijah and Elisha. But we should note that like Moses, Elijah was troubled by the burden of his work, notwithstanding the apparent triumph he had achieved on Mount Carmel.[19] Knowing that he was facing the wrath of Jezebel, and following God's own direction to him, Elijah had fled to Sinai.[20] Just as the mountain had trembled at the time of Moses,[21] so also it trembled at the time of Elijah, though in his case the voice of God was not found in the violence of the storm and earthquake, but in a low whisper.[22] At the time, Elijah was given three clear tasks: to anoint Hazael as king of Syria, Jehu as king of Israel and Elisha as his own successor as prophet. In the end, Elijah would carry out only the last of these commands himself, anointing Elisha his successor immediately after leaving Sinai, casting his cloak on him as a sign of the call.[23] The call of Elisha is very much like Jesus' call of the first disciples in Mark,[24] in that he acted as the prophet who called them to a specific ministry with him. Just as Jesus called his disciples to leave the security of their nets, so also Elisha was called to leave the security of his family's farm, even sacrificing the oxen in a special meal with his community.

In the account of Elijah and Elisha there are a number of clear echoes of the relationship between Moses and Joshua. Just as Moses found himself unable to complete his task in the face of the stubbornness of his people, so also Elijah's ministry would need to be carried on by another. It was Elisha who carried out the anointing of Jehu[25] and announced to Hazael that he would be king of Syria.[26] Unlike the relationship between Moses and Joshua, that of Elijah and Elisha was more consciously patterned on a discipleship model. But as Joshua did for

Moses, so Elisha acted as Elijah's assistant,[27] though the content of this role is not made clear. Indeed, we do not formally meet Elisha again until the account of Elijah's being taken up.[28] At the time of Elijah's transport, Elisha was permitted to receive the mantle that had been the sign of Elijah's office and had been cast over him at his call. This was not Elijah's decision – it was God's, because in this way God was able to publicly declare that Elisha was the one who would continue Elijah's ministry.

It is from this point that Elisha's discipleship comes to the fore, because it is here that we see God's goal in calling and training him, although its direction had already been made clear when God had directed Elijah to call him. Just as much of Elijah's ministry had been patterned on that of Moses, so also Elisha patterned his on Moses through Elijah. Many of Elisha's miracles essentially repeat those carried out by Elijah – both provide miraculous amounts of oil for widows[29] and both revive a dead son.[30] Other miracles performed by Elisha look more consciously back to Moses – just as Moses provided bread in the wilderness, so also Elisha was able to provide bread for the camp of the sons of the prophets.[31] As with Joshua, one could suggest that Elisha acted as he did because God provided the context, but it is also the case that Elisha consciously modelled his ministry on that of Moses, so that he also followed the pattern established by Joshua. Thus, in the context of fulfilling the call of his own ministry, Elisha follows the pattern established for him by Elijah, a pattern that reaches back through Joshua to Moses. But for both Elijah and Elisha, the crucial element was that ministry was shaped by discipleship, and it was the call of God that was central. In neither case do we find them engaged in a discipleship programme for its own sake: discipleship is only meaningful in the context of commitment to the ministry that God has laid out before them.

Conclusion

A great deal more could be said, yet it is clear that even though the technical terminology of discipleship occurs infrequently in the Old Testament, the actual practice does not. On the contrary, there are a number of important examples of discipling and discipleship in practice. What we see is not only the background to Jesus' practice but also some important insights into the very nature of discipleship. The point is not to distil these into a checklist of principles for discipleship today, nor to develop them into a model for discipleship relationships. The heart of these insights lies in the fact that discipleship is only meaningful when it is committed from the outset to the mission of God, committed to faithfully fulfilling the call placed on one's life by God. This is the framework that we see in the Old Testament, and also reflected in the New Testament as it describes the life and ministry of Jesus. In commissioning his followers to continue the pattern he has modelled,[32] Jesus is inviting them to be part of God's mission in bringing all things ultimately under the lordship of Christ.[33]

So it behoves us to reflect deeply on God's mission, to resist reducing it to a portfolio of set phrases or 'objectives' that are unable to shape our living and discipleship. Rather we are invited to immerse ourselves in the comprehensive nature of the salvation that God has initiated and will one day bring to consummation, a salvation that we see unfolding throughout the Scriptures. The more fully we grasp the scope of God's mission and his invitation to be part of it, the more deeply we will want our discipleship to help us to understand and then faithfully fulfil that calling. The Old Testament presents Moses as one who sets a pattern for others to follow, because in Moses we see a man committed to doing the will of God. That is why Moses is the pattern, not only for believers within the Old Testament, but also for Jesus himself.

♦ ♦ ♦ ♦

Further reading

Hutton, Rodney R., *Charisma and Authority in Israelite Society* (Fortress Press, 1994)

Kraus, H. J., *The People of God in the Old Testament* (Lutterworth, 1958)

Robinson, H. Wheeler, *The Cross in the Old Testament* (SCM, 1955)

Sheriffs, Deryck, *The Friendship of the Lord – An Old Testament Spirituality* (Paternoster, 1996)

von Rad, Gerhard, *Moses* (Lutterworth, 1960)

Wright, Christopher J. H., *Old Testament Ethics for the People of God* (IVP, 2004)

Notes

1 E.g. Mk. 1:16-20.

2 It is well known that prominent rabbis would also call their own disciples before the time of Jesus, but the same argument holds true for them – they could call disciples because the model was already understood in the Old Testament. Indeed, it will be seen that by reverting to a model of peripatetic discipleship, Jesus actually moved back towards the Old Testament pattern in a way that was not common amongst rabbis.

3 Is. 50:4 (twice); 54:13; Jer. 2:24; 13:23.

4 See chapter 5: The 'end' of discipleship.

5 Ex. 18; Num. 11:1-30.

6 Also Aaron and Hur.

7 Ex. 17:9-16.

8 Also translated 'minister'.
9 Ex. 32:17.
10 Ex. 33:7-11.
11 Num. 11:29.
12 Num. 13 – 14. Joshua is also referred to here (in 13:8) by his alternative name, Hoshea, though the fact of Moses' renaming him Joshua is recorded in 13:16. There is, perhaps, a parallel here with Jesus' renaming of Simon as Peter (Mt. 16:18).
13 Num. 27:18.
14 Num. 34:17.
15 Josh. 2.
16 Compare Josh. 3 – 4 with Ex. 14:21-31.
17 Ex. 12:1-28; Josh. 5:10-12.
18 Ex. 3:4-6; Josh. 5:13-15.
19 1 Kgs. 18.
20 1 Kgs. 19:8.
21 Ex. 19:18.
22 1 Kgs. 19:12. We should possibly translate as 'a thin silence'. In any case, the rebuke to Elijah was that he thought God was only active in the spectacular, but it is made clear to him here that this is not the case.
23 1 Kgs. 19:19-21.
24 Mk. 1:16-20.
25 2 Kgs. 9:1-13, though Elisha did this through one of the 'sons of the prophets'.
26 2 Kgs. 8:7-15.
27 1 Kgs. 19:21.
28 2 Kgs. 2:1-18.
29 1 Kgs. 17:8-16; 2 Kgs. 4:1-7.
30 1 Kgs. 17:17-24; 2 Kgs. 4:18-37; cf. Lk. 7:11-17.
31 Ex. 16; 2 Kgs. 4:42-44; cf. Mt. 14:13-21.
32 Mt. 28:19-20.
33 Col. 1:15-20.

3

Ephesians 4 ministries and spiritual formation

Greg Haslam

Greg was born in Liverpool and became a Christian there in 1967. In 1975 he graduated with a degree in Theology and History, and after teaching for three years he left to train for pastoral ministry. He was senior pastor at Winchester Family Church for twenty-one years. Greg travels widely both in the UK and overseas; he and his wife Ruth have a particular interest in India and have visited several times in connection with a growing church-plant there. Greg became minister of Westminster Chapel in March 2002.

In this chapter Greg explores the fivefold ministries of Ephesians 4 and their radical agenda for building up the people of God. He emphasises that it's in the context of Christian unity that God intended these ministries to function effectively in order to help God's people grow towards maturity and to equip them for the works he has prepared in advance for them to do.

For reflection

- How might the fivefold ministries equip Christians to be radical disciples in today's world?
- How will you respond to the challenges at the end of this chapter?

Ephesians 4 ministries and spiritual formation

Spiritual formation is nothing more nor less than the reversal of the Fall and the process that leads to the restoration of the broken image of God in human beings. God is in the business of recreating and renewing people's lives, imparting saving knowledge to them and, over time, dramatically transforming their thinking, character and living. We are all dependent on each other for the successful outcome of this process. God uses the direct power of his own Word and Spirit to effect these changes, but he rarely bypasses human agency in this transformation, for Christian leaders and mentors play a vital role also. Jesus said, 'A student is not above his teacher, but everyone who is fully trained will be like his teacher' (Lk. 6:40, NIV). We become like our mentors in every way. This is a process that involves information, impartation and imitation, i.e. personal growth in knowledge, skills and character.

I want to suggest that as we tackle this key question of assisting God's people to grow towards unity and maturity, helping them to become equipped for the works he has prepared in advance for them to do, the fivefold ministries of Ephesians 4 are crucial. Indeed, I want to suggest that one of the greatest single factors that could unite and accelerate the maturity of the church today would be the influence and spiritual authority of many emerging teams in which the diverse gifts of apostles, prophets, evangelists, pastors and teachers genuinely work together towards the goal of completing the body of Christ on earth as an effective agent of God in restoring all things. These fivefold ministries are Christ's gifts to his entire church throughout all time until the *parousia*; they are not just the monopoly of one sector of that church, or one period of time – the first century AD, for example.

The context of Christian unity

But to understand this fully we must look at these 'Ephesians 4 ministries' in context, allowing the whole of the apostle Paul's letter to the Ephesians to shape our understanding of how God intends these ministries to function effectively. Most significantly this means that Paul's understanding of Christian unity, the theme uppermost in his mind following his exploration of God's sovereign grace and purpose in chapters 1-3, is to govern their outworking. Sin has fragmented and disintegrated God's cosmos. The Gospel reorders and reintegrates it, and the prototype model of the Gospel's success is to be seen in the church. This is the governing idea of this Epistle.

But we must be clear. The unity Paul speaks of in this letter is not organisational or institutional, it is *organic*. It is a 'unity of the Spirit' (v.3). This is not 'union' – as someone once remarked about merely human organisation to this end, 'Putting two coffins side by side will not produce a resurrection.' Nor is it 'uniformity', the cloned and politicised 'unity' that marks some expressions of modern ecumenism – a mass of icebergs assembled into one huge continent of ice, just as cold, and just as dead. It is 'unanimity', or heart agreement and common witness that God alone can achieve by his Spirit (Rom. 15:5-7). This requires a mentoring process, in order to facilitate such a transformation, and Paul is modelling this even as he writes. He is discipling his readers in attitudinal adjustments, understanding and action.

Ephesians 4 ministries and character change (4:1-3)

Paul knows that there are genuine believers whom we feel both drawn to and distant from at the same time. So we're first summoned to desire and work hard for unity, knowing it will not be easily achieved: 'Make every effort,' he says (v.3). Paul calls us to cultivate three attitudinal changes to make this possible (vv.2-3).

1. *Instead of pride let there be humility (v.2a)*
   An air of superiority over doctrinal purity (Reformed evangelicals), historic ancestry ('Catholic' groupings), spiritual vitality (Charismatics and Pentecostals) or 'anointed' leadership authority ('Restoration' streams) is pride; it results in a refusal to network with those we consider 'inferior'. Humility helps us acknowledge our deficiencies and be genuinely grateful for the complementary strengths of others within the church, e.g. their theological legacy, ethical purity, social action, faith expectancy or church-planting success.

2. *Instead of harshness let there be gentleness (v.2b)*
   Harshness springs from either a defensive 'fortress' mentality or the selfish ambition to build 'our own little empire'. This must give way to a restraint and self-control that believes and speaks well of fellow-Christians.

3. *Instead of frustration let there be patience (v.2c)*
   Other Christians can intensely irritate us at times. They're often slow to see and believe what we clearly see, and we become impatient. The Elizabethan Puritans had a slogan, 'Reformation without tarrying for anybody', but we have to tarry!

Christ will bring the whole fragmented body into his end-time purposes, so that as with Israel at the Exodus, 'Not a hoof shall be left behind' (Ex. 10:26). God hasn't finished with us yet. We can afford to be patient as stragglers catch up with what others have seen, well in advance of them.

Ecclesiastical exclusiveness from others is ultimately self-defeating. We need each other. A passion for unity necessarily entails a larger-heartedness that gives expression to the familial love the Father has implanted in all our hearts by his Spirit.

Ephesians 4 ministries and fresh understanding (4:4-6)

The prophet complained, 'My people are destroyed from lack of knowledge' (Hos. 4:6, NIV). Paul models the art of conveying cognitive instruction as he develops his readers' knowledge and understanding, in order to persuade and motivate them to pursue unity. Though differences exist between believers, there is also a profound common ground that is more fundamental than the issues that divide us. The great essentials that Paul lists here (vv.4-6) express the complete sevenfold foundation for unity. All Christians share this in common. That is why each component is prefaced by the numeral 'one' – it undergirds our unity.

- *One Body*: The whole church is congenitally joined together like a human body. Geographical, cultural, and even minor doctrinal differences cannot affect this reality. So, 'what God has joined together, let no one separate.'

- *One Spirit*: Every believer has experienced the same spiritual power, since we're all 'born from above' (Jn. 3:2-7) and possessors of Christ's Spirit (Rom. 8:9), with access to the same supply of more, and able to 'drink of one Spirit' (1 Cor. 12:13). If the Holy Spirit seals someone as his own (Eph.1:13), then I am obliged to own them also.

And Paul's list goes on:

- *One Hope*: We will all unite in the same eschatological future destiny, so why not start practising now?
- *One Lord*: A fact that explains the serendipity we feel when we encounter other genuine believers. The Christ in me will not quarrel with the Christ in you.
- *One Faith*: Our common saving faith in God's saving Son is the focus of profound union for us all by his powerful grace.
- *One Baptism*: Dramatically depicting our death to sin and resurrection to unfragmented new creation in Christ.
- *One God and Father*: Our relationship with God is initiated and experienced through regeneration and adoption, which makes us all siblings in the same family of God whether we like it or not.

Louis Berkhof summarises the thrust of this passage:

> The Reformers argued that the body (referring to the invisible church) was controlled by one head, Jesus Christ, animated by one Spirit, the Spirit of Christ. This unity meant that all those who belong to the church

> share in the same faith, are cemented together by the common bond of love, and have the same glorious outlook upon the future.[1]

There are no valid rivals to these seven single components of true unity. Indeed, it is the false belief that there are rival alternatives that has fragmented humanity in the first place and continues to do so.

In short, Christian people, no matter how diverse in ethnicity, social status, speech, style, dress, culture or age, all share a unity in Christ that is more fundamental than any lesser issues which may serve to divide them. The Ephesians 4 ministries help us to grasp and know this. Facts are facts, and facts are stubborn things.

Ephesians 4 ministries and new skills (4:7-13)

In the light of this, it is obvious that the true unity of the church is as indestructible as the Godhead itself. We can no more split the church than we can split the Godhead. Yet the reality remains that our historical and existential situation appears very different. There are thirty thousand Christian denominations worldwide and the fragmentation continues. There are widespread manifestations of selfish ambition, protectionism, exclusivism, rivalry, mutual recrimination, ignorance, fear and strife.

The apostle therefore adds to his exhortation to grasp the right attitude and understanding about unity, the practical and existential processes by which unity is attained. He underscores the crucial role that the ministry gifts of the ascended Lord play in this. Their very diversity underlines the fact that in Paul's thought, unity does not equal uniformity. The church will ultimately display a diversity in unity like that of the Trinity itself, reflective of the kaleidoscopic grace of God (1 Pet. 4:10), and this involves the dynamic cooperation of three agencies in the perfecting and maturing process leading to one great and glorious outcome:

1. The ascended Lord
2. The anointed ministry gifts of the ascended Christ
3. Issuing in the every-member ministry of the whole body of Christ
4. And the result? – An end-time glorious church on earth

1. The ascended Lord – the donor of ministry (vv.7-11)
As authoritative ruler at the right hand of God it is Christ who calls, commissions and equips his followers. He alone is *the* Apostle (Heb. 3:1), Prophet (Lk. 24:19; Jn. 4:19), Evangelist (Mk. 1:15), Pastor (Jn. 10:14) and Teacher (Mt. 7:28; Jn. 13:13). Yet in these anointed ministries also, we encounter the same powerful expressions of Christ's own words, works and wonders as he deploys them to extend his kingdom and build his church. Their appearance challenges both existing leaders and whole churches to recognise and receive them as Christ's gifts to advance our progress towards his eschatological goals. This is why Christ sends them.

2. The anointed ministry gifts of the ascended Christ – existing in a wide diversity (v.11)
Please note the time reference 'until' in verse 13. This indicates the continuous donation of them to his church until the climax of history, not their cessation at some time earlier, as some have maintained is the case. These goals have not been attained yet; the means must still be

available. Christ's own ministry skills are in effect divided among the individuals listed. Perhaps the most controversial are the apostles and prophets.

a) *Apostles*. The word 'apostle' (from the noun *apostolos* – 'sent one', and its related verb *apostello* – 'to send') means one who is sent to represent and exercise authority on behalf of another, carrying a kind of ambassadorial status for a superior who cannot personally be present. It carries different senses in different contexts in the New Testament. The early church fully understood that certain individuals were commissioned by Christ to spread the Gospel and found healthy churches, in order to ensure its preservation and expansion in a geographical area. There are five kinds of apostle in the New Testament:

1. *Jesus, the Chief Apostle* – there is no one like him (Heb. 3:1: 'The apostle and high priest of our confession'). All other ministries only share a small measure of his gifting and ability, by the Spirit.
2. *The foundational twelve apostles of the Lamb* (Rev. 21:14) – these accompanied Christ for three years during his earthly ministry and became eyewitnesses of his resurrection, and in some cases wrote Scripture – there are none like them today (Acts 1:22, Rev. 21:14). Interestingly, Matthias joined this select company as a replacement for Judas Iscariot (Acts 1:23).
3. *Paul, the thirteenth apostle* – the 'last of all, as to one untimely born' (1 Cor. 15:8). He shared equal authority with the twelve (Gal. 1:15-17, 2:9; Eph. 3:8), and also wrote inspired Scripture as the definitive standard of teaching for the church. No apostle today has this stature or function. But Paul was also a 'bridge' apostle and a model for later

individuals who became 'apostolic' missionary church-planters, since he was distinctly called by the ascended Lord to model this task among the Gentiles (Gal. 2:7-9).

4. *Pioneer church planters* – who, like Paul, make new converts, plant churches, lay foundations of life and doctrine, decide matters of controversy or conduct, and generally set things in order (1 Cor. 3:10; Acts 15:1-2, 23; 2 Thess. 3:6-8; 1 Cor. 11:14; Tit. 1:5, etc.). Paul did this of course, but also taught others to do the same, and so he not only belatedly completed the small circle of 'apostles of the resurrected Lord' as eyewitnesses of his resurrection, he also launched a new series of 'apostles of the ascended Christ', many of whom are named in the New Testament and who were not part of the twelve. These travelled together, usually in teams, and included individuals like Barnabas, Silas, Timothy, Titus, James the Lord's brother, and possibly Junias and Andronicus (Rom. 16:7).
5. *Any Christian sent anywhere to do anything, as an envoy of the church* – e.g. Epaphroditus, who was 'sent' to represent the Philippians as Paul's servant in Rome (Phil. 2:25). Many are sent on special errands like this by churches today. The context alone determines the meaning and use of the term 'apostle'.

b) *Prophets*. The role of the prophet is also a word-based ministry that builds hope amongst people and brings revelation, insight, exhortation and transcendent guidance to the church that is not available by ordinary, natural means. Agabus, Judas and Silas are fine examples (Acts 11:27-28; 21:10-11). The Holy Spirit imparts verbal and visual information to their spirits in words, warnings, visions, dreams, impressions and symbolic actions that stir hope and movement in God's people. The apostle Paul instructs us in how to covet, practise and pastor this ministry, and also to esteem their utterances if genuine and properly tested by Scripture. Prophetic words stand under the authority of scriptural revelation, not over it, and should be honoured if truly beneficial (1 Cor. 14:3, 37-38; 1 Thess. 5:19-22). Walter Brueggemann writes, 'The task of prophetic ministry is to nurture, nourish and evoke a consciousness and perception alternative to the consciousness and perception of the dominant culture around us.'[2] And Hans Kung believes, 'A Church in which prophets have to keep silent declines and becomes a spiritless organisation.' It's good for churches to ask, 'Is there a prophet in the house?' Mostly, the church has become a non-prophet organisation!

c) *Evangelists*. These spearhead the church's outreach into the unbelieving community and equip others to do the same. They broadcast the evangel and persuade others to come to faith in Christ by proclamation and demonstration of its kingdom power in both words and deeds. We should expect social change and signs and wonders to accompany their ministry (Mk. 16:15-20; Acts 8:4-8). And finally,

d) and e) *Pastors and teachers*. It's unclear whether Paul refers to one or two distinct ministries here. Both have special abilities to influence people's lives by their counsel, care and teaching of the Word of God in the power of the Spirit, privately and in public. They feed, guide, mature, protect and lead new converts by their ability to patiently expound and wisely apply Scripture, as they instruct, admonish, discipline and train whole churches to become healthy and influential.

We can summarise the contribution of the range of word-ministries delineated here in this way: *apostles govern, prophets guide, evangelists gather, pastors guard and teachers ground* the church in the whole of God's revealed truth. In Acts, all five ministries travelled and worked together in flexible mix-and-match teams, launching churches and also helping them develop (Acts 13:1-2; 15:22-34; 16:1-10; 17:1; 18:5, 27, etc.). Since this is the model for all time, it is entirely appropriate that we should look towards the formation of varied 'apostolic teams' of gifted individuals operating among denominations worldwide. We should honour them whenever and wherever they appear. We ignore them to our loss or even at our peril.

The greatest single factor that could unite and accelerate the maturity of the church today would be to recognise and benefit from the influence and spiritual authority of these translocal ministries. God authorises and empowers them to disciple and equip others, giving them the necessary permission and power to change people's beliefs and behaviour in line with the will of God. Without their influence, people's lives will remain deficient, endangered and underdeveloped.

Their function is clearly not to promote themselves or even to form an organisation or 'ministry' centred on an individual alone. It is to take their place within flexible networks or teams of similarly gifted servants, for higher ends. The Bible says, 'Two are better than one' (Ecc. 4:9-12), and Jesus sent the first apostles out 'two by two', and later did the same with the seventy-two (Lk. 9:1-6, 10:1ff). Paul rarely chose to work alone, and travelled with individuals such as Barnabas, Mark, Silas, Timothy, Luke, Priscilla and Aquila and scores of others. In the New Testament, 'leadership' is clearly a collective noun.[3]

Individualism, independence and isolation are therefore quick routes to error or imbalance in belief and behaviour. They also hamper the discipling of the church. Without this diversity of mentoring influence, the full development of the body is impaired. Teachers functioning alone tend to produce passive lovers of doctrine; evangelists may gather large numbers of spiritual babies who may remain immature. Lone prophets may only fire a handful of fanatical and visionary enthusiasts, whilst pastors operating in isolation may cultivate only a flock of well-taught but inward-looking, bloated and smugly contented sheep! Exposure to the diversity of Christ's word-ministries, however, brings balance and new perspective to individuals and whole congregations.

3. These ministries equip the whole church to function properly (vv.12-13)

These complementary giftings ensure that Jesus in the totality of his fivefold ministry is free to address his life-changing word to the totality of his body upon earth. No one person possesses all that is necessary to bring the church to maturity. Neither does any single stream or team. To ignore or silence ministries which the Lord providentially puts our way is to defraud the church of some aspect of Christ's ministry to her. Vital emphases will be shut out. Welcomed, these dynamic ministries will advance us towards God-ordained goals. They are 'to prepare God's people for works of service' (v.12a, NIV), operating both in the church and also for the benefit of our needy world – for there is nothing 'secular' except sin!

The effect of exposure to these fivefold ministries is that apostles make us more 'apostolic' and mission-minded; prophets impart the ability to prophesy and to become future-oriented and filled with hopeful optimism; evangelists not only win the lost themselves but also stir and train us to become more evangelistic and skilled in that task ourselves; pastors cause us to become caring and familial in our community life together – the 'wow' factor that outsiders quickly notice; and teachers awaken our appetite for truth, deepening our faith theologically so that we are characterised by an informed biblicism and doctrinal accuracy. These effects are wonderful and highly desirable – especially at this present time of fragmentation, immaturity and weakness in much of the church.

4. The result – an end-time glorious church (vv.13-16)

We are to become the vanguard display of God's ultimate plan for the whole of the cosmos! As translocal ministries ignore denominational boundaries and cross-fertilise different congregations, they will help break up the lonely, isolated and in some cases fiercely independent ethos of many Christian groupings. It is because such ministries have hitherto been comparatively scarce, barely recognised and frequently unwelcome that the church has remained ill-taught, ill-equipped, numerically small, immature and vulnerable to deception. It is futile to long and pray for unity and expanding mission whilst at the same time disparaging the instruments God uses to effect this.

Ephesians tells us that we are headed towards four divinely appointed ends within the purpose of God.

1. *Unity in the faith and in the knowledge of the Son of God (v.13a)*
   That is, unanimity and commitment to the essentials of the apostolic faith revealed in the Bible (Rom. 15:5-7).

2. *Maturity: attaining to the whole measure of the fullness of Christ (vv.13b, 15)*
   Infancy is a condition of untapped and underdeveloped potential. To grow up is to move towards a full expression of all that Jesus has imparted to us by reason of our union with him. On earth he had power to preach with authority, heal and deliver with dramatic effect, make groups of radical converts and cement them together in community, then launch them to speak prophetically to the 'principalities and powers' of his day. A mature church will do the same today.
3. *Stability: no longer easily unsettled by false teaching (vv.14-15)*
   Infancy is a time when convictions are held lightly and there is vulnerability to deception. Children are fooled by trickery and charm, ostentation and show. The present-day kindergarten of 'baby' Christians still learning their ABC will yield to a vast company of biblically well informed men and women who know what they believe and can ably defend it.
4. *Ministry: the whole body functioning together as each part does its work (v.16)*
   Isolated and maverick ministry will give way to a fresh understanding of our interdependence upon one another. At present the body of Christ is not healthy. Muscles are paralysed, limbs hang useless and vital organs malfunction. In some quarters we appear to be in a critical condition. The church can indeed fully function again. But will this happen?

The answer to this depends to a large extent upon our individual and corporate response to the overall challenges presented above.

1. Are we willing to pay any price, as Paul himself was, to see the goal of Christian unity come closer to realisation through our own influence and personal sacrifice?
2. Do we need to repent of any past pride, harshness and impatience displayed towards other members of the body of Christ?
3. Will we resolve to honour the impact and witness of every genuine Christian congregation and effective leader we know of, and be willing to demolish some of the barriers to fellowship with them?
4. Will we permit our own life and ministry to be mentored by good relationships with any genuine apostolic, prophetic, evangelistic, pastoral and teaching ministries Christ sends us?
5. In effective partnership with others will we make it our goal to use whatever gifts Christ has given us to equip others for their works of service wherever God has called them?

How will we, and how will you, respond to these challenges?

Until such ministries are again heard and seen in action among us, we may remain somewhat handicapped and indefinitely stunted, never reaching our full potential. God help us if that should ever be the case.

♦ ♦ ♦ ♦

Further reading

Conner, Kevin J., *The Church in the New Testament* (Bible Temple Publishing, 1982)

Connor, Mark, *Transforming Your Church* (Sovereign World, 2000)

Eaton, Michael, *Enjoying God's Worldwide Church* (Sovereign World, 1995)

Greenslade, Philip, *Leadership – Reflections on Biblical Leadership Today* (CWR, 2002)

Virgo, Terry, *A People Prepared* (Kingsway, 1996)

Virgo, Terry, *Does the Future Have a Church?* (Kingsway, 2003)

Wagner, Peter C., *Churchquake!* (Regal, 1999)

Notes

1. Louis Berkhof, *Systematic Theology* (The Banner of Truth Trust, 1996).
2. Walter Brueggemann, *The Prophetic Imagination* (Fortress Press, 1978).
3. See also chapter 9: What are leaders for?

Wisdom from earlier generations,
wisdom for today

4

From darkness to light: lessons in disciple-making from our great-grandparents in Christ

Martyn Atkins

Martyn is a Methodist minister and Principal of Cliff College in Derbyshire. He is author of several books, including Preaching in a Cultural Context. *He lectures in mission and evangelism in the UK and various institutions around the world and is presently researching future shapes of the church.*

In this chapter Martyn describes the process of disciple-making prevalent in the early church that was known as catechesis. He identifies ways in which the characteristics of the pre-modern world in which the early church functioned have significant parallels in our twenty-first-century UK culture. He then goes on to suggest that a culturally appropriate implementation of catechesis may once again be God's anointed tool for disciple-making.

For reflection

- How might the idea of catechesis help you to think through the process of growing as a disciple?
- If you were to devise a simple catechesis for your church, what would it look like?

From darkness to light: lessons in disciple-making from our great-grandparents in Christ

This article contends for something straightforward yet challenging. Namely, that a crucial means by which authentic, mature disciples of Jesus Christ will be made in the west in the early twenty-first century will come through appropriately revising and innovatively implementing the distinctive way of making disciples developed in the early centuries of Christianity. This was known as catechesis.

Catechesis: what is it?

Catechesis was the term given to a comprehensive process of disciple-making popular in the early centuries of Christianity. Various models of catechesis were developed over the first four centuries. Nevertheless 'classic' catechesis involved several discernible phases, beginning with the enquiry of a 'seeker' and ending with a mature, fully initiated Christian. I sketch out here a somewhat rosy and romantic, but nonetheless essentially accurate, composite picture of early church catechesis.[1]

Gathering seekers
'Enquirers' or 'seekers' (yes, the Christian ancients did use that phrase – it isn't an invention of Willow Creek!) were gathered together in a group and shared in what might now be regarded as 'pre-evangelism'. Seekers were welcomed by the leader (the catechist) and introduced to each other and to some Christians who also shared in the group. The balance of seekers and Christians was carefully thought out. Seekers and Christians alike were provided with opportunities to

share stories of emerging faith. These narratives were often used to point out the leading of God in their lives. Seekers were seeking, they were told, because of God's prevenient work in their lives through the Spirit. It was providence, not coincidence, that brought them to this point.

In this way they were exhorted to begin the pilgrimage of faith in earnest, and at this point probably began spiritual practices and disciplines such as praying, fasting, repentance and forgiveness. They shared worship in the group, but not yet public worship with believers. This first phase – technically termed the 'pre-catechumenate' – often ended with a special ritualised event, giving opportunity for individuals to continue or withdraw with dignity.

Growing catechumens

Next was a lengthy process of further enquiry and instruction. We must not put enlightenment heads on pre-enlightenment shoulders, but it is clear that there was more to catechesis than being taught doctrine. Yes, they were taught the faith; yes, they did read and receive exposition of the Scriptures; yes, the role of the catechist was vital. But notions of boring third-century confirmation classes must be dispelled. There appears to have been an emphasis on experience and encounter, on turning from evil and holding fast to God in Christ. There was discovery and dialogue, prayer and purgation, openness and obedience. There was rite and ritual, rote and rigour. It was as if the whole person – soul, mind and body – was being engaged. Through this came the repeated invitation to believe: this meant commitment to Christ, his people the church, the imitation of his lifestyle and the taking up of the life of faith.

Preparing the 'elect'

At a certain point in the process the mood moved from exploration to preparation. The catechumens began to be referred to as the 'elect' and spiritual preparation began in a new and earnest way for serious Christian commitment, ritualised and sealed supremely in baptism. Prayer, fasting and ritual exorcisms increased (often over the period of Lent), ending in a joyful, serious, 'public' baptism when, for the first time, the believer took his or her place in the congregation of the faithful and shared fully in corporate worship, including Holy Communion.

Developing disciples

Some models of catechesis stop at baptism, but many don't. These outline a continuing context of sharing and teaching (known as 'post-' or 'mystagogical' catechesis) and further integration into the main congregation. Throughout Christian history the transition of believers from small, intimate groupings into larger congregations has entailed sensitivity and skill. At this point the believers would be encouraged to exercise the gifting and talents identified and sanctified through the catechetical process, for the good of the church. For the first time, the baptised believers were referred to as 'disciples'.[2]

Catechesis: why is it so important today?

Some readers will have found this account of historic catechesis interesting in its own right. Others will not. 'What has all this got to do with making disciples now, in the twenty-first century?' they ask. A good question, to which I believe there are several good answers.

It is a tool for post-Christendom, as it was for pre-Christendom

Catechesis appears to be a chosen, even anointed, tool for making Christian disciples *in a time of cultural transition*. It was at its most useful and effective in the context of 'in-betweenness', a period when the church was moving from the margins of Roman society – weak, misunderstood, sometimes despised – towards a place near the heart of Roman society: powerful, influential and respected. Put more technically, catechesis was a profoundly influential instrument for evangelism, conversion, nurture and discipling during the transition from pre-Christendom to the origins of Christendom.[3]

Today we are at the other end of the Christendom enterprise. Scholars and theologians of all sorts of persuasion talk about the lengthening shadows of Christendom, the end of the dominant role of the western church and its faith as unquestioned public truth. Many now talk of 'post-Christendom' to signal, in a variety of ways, the move of Christianity back to the margins of influence, the periphery of importance, witnessed by the fact that it is effectively ignored by a huge proportion of our population.[4]

In short, though of course there are differences, there are more than enough similarities and resonances to suggest that the principles enshrined in ancient catechesis are ripe for reappropriation. I believe its time has come again.

Catechesis made disciples in religiously plural contexts

After centuries of assumptions about 'Christian Europe' and 'Christian Britain', itself the language of Christendom, the present and increasing religious and cultural plurality of the west is regarded by some as a fall from grace. Perhaps it is. It is salutary to realise, however, that the early church lived naturally in a context of great plurality. Catechesis operated effectively when Christianity was not a religious monopoly, or the assumed faith default position. Catechesis was the means whereby people became disciples as they lived cheek by jowl with people of all sorts of faiths and belief systems.

This religiously plural context included not only some 'formal religions' (the equivalents of Islam and Hinduism today) but also, importantly, 'implicit' religious systems, the close equivalents of New Age and New Paganism today. I recall the impact *The Faith of the Unbeliever*[5] made upon me when I read it in the mid-1990s. It was this book that first convinced me not only of the slow demise of Christendom Christianity, but also of the related need to take seriously the pervasive nature of unbelief that largely filled the gap.

Unbelief was not non-belief. Rather an 'unbeliever . . . is not someone who does not believe in God' but one 'who has chosen to step outside of the Christian tradition either to express an informal faith or to celebrate having no particular religious faith.'[6] The notion of Christian Britain was blown apart. The persistent folklore that if the church got its act together, made worship more relevant, played the right music, heated the sanctuary, ripped out the pews and the like, hordes of folk would gratefully return was rejected for the myth it is. Instead, the unbelievers of Britain need engaging with strategies for mission and witness as robust and thought-through as those for any other faith system. Traditional (Christendom) models of evangelism, confirmation training and so on seem increasingly unrelated to such a situation. Catechesis, as the means whereby Christian disciples were made in a religiously plural environment not unlike our own in the west today, takes on new possibilities and potentials.

Catechesis worked effectively when there was little Christian knowledge or church experience

Catechesis took place in an environment in which few people had any real knowledge or experience of the Christian faith, or had quirky or inadequate impressions of it. It assumed very little about a seeker other than that they were seeking. When preparing for baptism, the catechist asked the candidates something like this: 'When you first sought the Way you did not know what you sought. You did not know the light of Christ, the truth of God, the illumination of the Spirit. Now you do. You have been taught it, experienced it and invited to live in it. Now I ask you, do you want to become a Christian, a disciple of the Lord Jesus Christ?'

Contrast this with (Christendom) assumptions about commitment and belief. Someone turns up for worship three weeks running and within a month they are a property steward! Why? Because we readily assume they are 'returning' to faith. Or again, contrast this approach with regular assumptions about evangelism. The great Billy Graham stood in British football stadiums and told folk, 'You know you have failed God . . . turned away from Christ . . . rejected the faith of your childhood. . . . I want you to get out of your seats . . .' He called people *back*, and in the dying embers of Christendom that made perfect sense. But we are not there now. Now, in the vast majority of cases, we would be calling people to return to nothing.

Catechesis, therefore, starting further back, assuming very little, taking longer, is a better process of making disciples in our increasingly post-Christendom culture.

Catechesis worked well in a variety of contexts and among different sorts of people

We tend to assume that the early church was homogeneous, all the same. It wasn't. Christianity in Africa, Syria, Rome or Jerusalem was quite different. Catechetical processes seemed able to work successfully in these quite different places. In the fourth century AD 'full blown' systems of catechesis were developed by Cyril of Jerusalem and Ambrose of Milan: east and west, and in significant respects, different worlds. Yet authentic Christian disciples were made in both contexts through the processes of catechesis which, while certainly orthodox and classically Christian, also reflected the different cultures and needs of the candidates in both places, and as such were quite dissimilar at various points.

It is also worth noting that besides being found in a wide variety of places, catechesis enabled disciples to be created among the rich and poor, educated and uneducated, slaves and free, the somebodies and the nobodies. Christians were made in cities and in villages, in settled times and in periods of persecution, among men and women and young and old. Catechesis, it appears, was just what is so desperately required today: a robust, orthodox, transferable and contextual means of making Christian disciples among a 'rainbow' population of different ages, stages and phases.

Catechesis worked because it was holistic and multifaceted

At least since the Enlightenment, the age of reason (beginning in earnest in the later seventeenth century), what it means to believe and profess Christian faith has gone through a process of reduction.[7] Not a reduction as in cooking, where the flavour of the sauce gets stronger;

more a reduction in terms of dilution, where something gets weaker and less distinct. The result is that Christian belief, for many, consists of nothing more than a series of mental assents to various doctrinal statements. This mentality permits the understandable but essentially inadequate practice of leading those who respond to evangelistic appeals through a few 'spiritual laws', and then, when assent to these is given, declaring the 'convert' to be a Christian. The mindset of modernist Christianity has been essentially cerebral.

Catechesis stands in sharp contrast to this reductionist view of believing. The whole person was involved, not just the head. All the senses were engaged. There was passivity and reception, decision and action. A healthy balance between believing, belonging and behaving was attempted because in catechesis they were all of a piece; each signalled the authenticity of the others. The equally important balance between individuality and corporate identity, between personal freedom and social responsibility, is evident in catechetical processes. It included opportunities for self-reflection, decision-making and decision-marking, personal development, chosen obedience and instruction. In a sentence, catechesis took whole human beings wholly seriously: their complexities, grandeur and sinfulness, potential and pitfalls. Above all there was an explicit reliance on the work of the Holy Spirit, without whose presence and infilling, through convicting, converting, enabling and accompanying, all else was regarded as folly.

Catechesis worked well because it took time

The evocative phrase used by ancient catechists to describe the process they facilitated is 'from darkness to light'. When one reads their accounts of catechesis the crude image of someone being 'cleaned out' comes to mind. It is as if the process engages the darkness of paganism, sucks a little of it out, then fills the space with the light of the Gospel through rituals of cleansing and freeing. This process, repeated over time and culminating in baptism and communion, brought a person ritually and spiritually from darkness to light. This clearly took time and in our I-want-it-all-and-I-want-it-now society it stands as a salutary lesson that good things cannot all come quickly. Both would-be disciples and the churches that disciple them will have to revise their estimates of the time, effort and sacrifice involved.

In recent years I have become an Emmaus Road person as much as a Damascus Road one. I think it normally takes time for humans to become Christians. I do not doubt that God can and does 'zap' human beings; I've been zapped a time or two myself. But equally I have little doubt that becoming a Christian is a journey, like the Emmaus story, with its evocative imagery of taking from morning till night. It is not that conversion is *either* crisis *or* process; it is that conversion *is* a process in which there *are* points of crisis. The whole makes for discipleship. The mistake of much evangelism is not that it stresses the significance of being 'born again' but that it equates such vital points of crisis with the complete nature of Christian conversion and discipleship.[8]

I suggest it takes about three years, at least, to get to grips with becoming a Christian. Some would say much longer. Catechists such as Tertullian, Cyril and Ambrose knew this. The full-blown process of discipling they outline takes about three years.

Some years ago John Finney interviewed about five hundred people who had recently professed Christian faith in some public way. He observed that on average it took between three and four years from someone's initial personal interest in Christian faith to the point of formal profession of that faith.[9]

If Finney relayed how to open the front door of the church a little wider, Philip Richter and Leslie Francis related how the back door of the church might be closed a little firmer. Their research into why people leave church today suggested that they did not wake up on a Tuesday morning and declare to the world, 'I'm giving up church'. Rather, people went through a process of 'deconversion' that, though no firm time-scale was given, suggested a small number of years from the point of initial disaffection to complete severing of the ties.[10]

It seems that it takes humans some time to truly change their mind. Faith development theorists have long known this. They suggest we move through faith stages throughout our lives. We do not all move at the same speed, or in the same direction, but many experts are agreed that for a person to make a decision to change at a profound level takes a period of something like three to four years.[11]

One is led inevitably to the conclusion that some two millennia ago the supreme catechist, a young Jewish rabbi who gathered twelve disciples round him and trained and mentored them for about three years, knew exactly what he was doing.

Catechesis: pre-modern discipling for postmodern disciples

In 1981 David Watson made a characteristically passionate and telling analysis of our current situation. '*Discipleship* sums up Christ's plan for the world,' he wrote.[12] Yet for all its brilliant simplicity, it is the one approach that most western churches have neglected.

Instead we have reports, commissions, conferences, seminars, missions, crusades, reunion schemes, liturgical reforms – the lot. But very little attention has been given to discipleship.

Catechesis gave full attention to discipleship. Its primary aim was a holistic and healthy experience that included seeking, repentance, forgiveness, conversion, salvation, liberation, teaching, cleansing, committing, believing, belonging, behaving, renewal, infilling, refilling. Such is needed today. Through Alpha, Emmaus, Christianity Explored, Disciple, RCIA, Essence and the like we are beginning to see the beginnings of catechesis, and its possibilities. But more is needed if authentic disciples are to be made in our present post-Christendom context, with its heady mixture of challenge and potential. An appropriate revision and innovative implementation of catechesis may once again be God's anointed tool for discipleship.

♦ ♦ ♦ ♦

Further reading

Finn, Thomas M., *From Death to Rebirth – Ritual and Conversion in Antiquity* (Paulist Press, 1997)

Fowler, James W., *Stages of Faith* (HarperCollins, 1995, paperback edition)

Kreider, Alan, *The Change of Conversion and the Origin of Christendom* (Trinity Press International, 1999)

Murray, Stuart, *Post-Christendom* (Paternoster, 2004)

Notes

1 One of the best accounts of ancient catechesis is Thomas M. Finn, *From Death to Rebirth – Ritual and Conversion in Antiquity* (Paulist Press, 1997).

2 A helpful outline of these stages is found in *The Study of Liturgy*, edited by C. Jones, G. Wainwright, E. Yarnold and P. Bradshaw (SCM, 1992), 127ff.

3 This is illustrated wonderfully in Alan Kreider, *The Change of Conversion and the Origin of Christendom* (Trinity Press International, 1999).

4 See Stuart Murray, *Post-Christendom* (Paternoster, 2004).

5 Martin Robinson, *The Faith of the Unbeliever* (Monarch, 1994).

6 Ibid., 93.

7 See William Abraham, *The Logic of Evangelism* (Eerdmans, 1989), especially chapter 1.

8 A helpful overview of contemporary approaches to initiation is the report from the General Synod of the Church of England, *On the Way: Towards an Integrated Approach to Christian Initiation* (Church House Publishing, 1995).

9 John Finney, *Finding Faith Today – How Does it Happen?* (British and Foreign Bible Society, 1992).

10 Philip Richter and Leslie Francis, *Gone but not Forgotten – Church Leaving and Returning* (Darton Longman & Todd, 1998), particularly chapter 2.

11 See, for example, the work of Jim Fowler, especially *Stages of Faith* (HarperCollins, 1995, paperback edition) and *Becoming Adult, Becoming Christian* (Harper and Row, 1984).

12 David Watson, *Discipleship* (Hodder & Stoughton, 1981).

5

The 'end' of discipleship: John Wesley's vision of real Christianity

Philip R. Meadows

Director of Postgraduate Studies at Cliff College in Derbyshire, Phil is an ordained presbyter in the British Methodist Church. He was lecturer in theology and religious studies at Westminster College, Oxford, before spending six years as E. Stanley Jones Professor of Evangelism at Garrett-Evangelical Theological Seminary, near Chicago, in the USA. He specialises in Wesley studies, missiology and the theology of evangelism; and is currently president of the Wesleyan Theological Society. His research and publication interests seek to combine theology and discipleship in the Wesleyan tradition with the missionary challenges of contemporary culture.

Wesley has made an excellent guru for scholars and leaders in search of general principles and universal techniques for ministry. But the heart of what Wesley has for us today lies in his compelling vision of the Christian life itself. It was his vision of forming a holy people, capable of being a living witness to the Gospel in uncertain times, that captured his imagination and directed his own search for 'whole-life discipleship'.

For reflection

- What vision of the Christian life captures your imagination?
- Is it capable of inspiring the development of disciple-making practices that will lead to a life-transforming relationship with God and with the world?

The 'end' of discipleship: John Wesley's vision of real Christianity

Why would twenty-first-century Christians turn to an eighteenth-century Anglican priest for inspiration about mission, evangelism and making disciples in our contemporary culture? In the case of John Wesley, the answer may seem obvious. He was the founder of a movement that grew from a few young men, meeting together in an Oxford University study-room, to a nationwide connexion of evangelical 'societies', and eventually into a major international denomination.

The rapid expansion of early Methodism might inspire us to examine Wesley's life and ministry as an example of 'effective' Christian leadership. We could examine his career as an itinerant evangelist, with the apostolic vocation of proclaiming the Gospel and planting new Christian communities among 'unchurched' people. We could examine the 'charismatic' and revivalistic nature of his evangelism as a reminder that we depend upon the supernatural power of the Holy Spirit for making disciples. We could examine his fascination with the early church and 'primitive Christianity' as a precursor to the 'ancient-future' church movement and our current fascination with radical and emerging ecclesiologies. We could observe his organisational genius for clues about how to gather people into small groups, connect them in local societies and bind them together in communicative networks. Or we could regard his commitment to mutual accountability in the formation of disciplined Christian fellowship as a model for making disciples.

Yet we could follow any of the above lines of enquiry, and more, and be liable to miss that which precedes them all: Wesley's compelling vision of the Christian life itself. This vision, which he called 'Christian perfection', captivated his imagination, reordered his desires and directed his own spiritual quest for 'whole-life discipleship'. It is my view that early Methodism really grew out of Wesley's own pursuit of holiness in heart and life, as his spiritual vision came to be shared with others and as they gathered together to help one another seek it. This common vision and common life began in the 'Holy Club' at Oxford, and spread from there through the formation, multiplication and connection of societies across the nation. Wesley and his preachers considered Christian perfection to be 'the grand depositum' of Methodism, and the self-avowed end of the movement was 'to spread scriptural holiness throughout the land'. Whatever Wesley thought or said or did, it was inspired, shaped and directed by the end of forming a holy people who, in the pursuit of perfection, were capable of being a living witness to the Gospel in uncertain times.

A vision worth staking our lives upon

The very talk of 'perfection' will no doubt fill many readers with dread! On the one hand, the Latin word *perfectio,* from which the English word 'perfection' comes, has the meaning of absolute metaphysical or divine perfection, being without defect of any kind. On the other hand, our technological culture has predisposed us to think of perfection in terms of absolute efficiency, flawless functionality, and being equally incapable of either failure or improvement. Clearly, both divine perfection and technological perfection are states quite beyond the reach of human attainment. Moreover, the expectations of such perfection – either self-imposed or required by others – are experienced as a burden too great for any of us to bear. Far from calling forth a life of virtue and excellence, holding out the goal of such perfection is more likely to engender disillusion, despondency and despair. We are right to be wary of striving for perfection.

Wesley, however, draws his terms from certain key texts in the King James Version of the Bible which translate the Greek word *teleios,* meaning the goal of Christian discipleship, in terms of 'perfection' (cf. Eph. 4:13; Phil. 3:15; Heb. 6:1; and 1 Jn. 4:18). He was a student of New Testament Greek and would have known that *teleios,* in these texts, meant being complete or fully-grown in the Christian life. Indeed, he insisted that Christian perfection was not an absolute perfection (*perfectio*), in either the divine or the technological sense, but the goal or end (*telos*) of a life aiming at spiritual maturity (*teleios*) understood in scriptural terms. It is a scriptural doctrine to strive after this 'perfection' or maturity because the character of spiritual maturity is itself the summation of scriptural injunctions about the Christian life.

Above all, Christian perfection is perfection in love (1 Jn. 4:18), a fulfilment of the Great Commandment to love God and neighbour (Mt. 22:36-39). Wesley describes it as the fullness of God's own loving presence and power overflowing in our love of neighbour, and thus returning to God in joyful prayer and thankful praise. As such, Christian perfection is not an accomplished state of being, but a dynamic way of life which flows from the most intimate and life-transforming relationship with God and extends to one's neighbour in mutual love and service. This life cannot be procured and possessed by our own ingenuity but is the gift of God's own life imparted to us, and Christ's own virtues reproduced in us, by the work of the Holy Spirit. In short, it is to have the mind which was in Christ (Phil. 2:5) and to walk as Christ walked.

Christian perfection is to have a heart and life fully renewed in the image of God (Rom. 8:29; 2 Cor. 3:18; Col. 3:10). It is a personal holiness that comes from our moment-to-moment dependence upon Christ as Prophet (shedding his light on the way), as Priest (offering his forgiveness along the way) and as King (supplying his strength for the way). It is, therefore, founded upon a *humility* that celebrates all our holiness to be dependent upon the work of Christ *for us* in reconciling us to God, and the work of his Spirit *in us* enabling the law of love to be fulfilled. This humility is inseparable from a *faith* that sees God's providence in all things, a *hope* that takes communion with God as our true end, and a *love* that unites us with God in time and eternity (1 Cor. 13). Christian perfection is, therefore, a life shaped by the *fruit* of the Spirit (Gal. 5:22) and the *witness* of the Spirit (Rom. 8:14-16), filled with the peaceful assurance of our acceptance as children of God through the merits of Christ, and of the Spirit's power to keep us from all sin.

For Wesley, the primary marks of this perfection in love are rejoicing always, praying without ceasing, and giving thanks in all circumstances (1 Thess. 5:16-18). The constancy and ubiquity of such joyful prayer and thankful praise belong to those whose hearts are ordered by love alone and whose minds are fixed upon God alone, whose thinking, speaking, feeling and acting are ruled exclusively by the love of God and neighbour. The pursuit of Christian perfection, or 'holiness in heart and life', is Wesley's language for 'whole-life discipleship'. It is a spiritual maturity that describes not only a *fullness* of God's love, reordering all our self-centred and worldly desires, but a *completeness* of devotion and dedication to God's will in every aspect of our lives. Perfection in love is embodied in *works of piety* – including all kinds of prayer, searching the Scriptures, receiving the Lord's Supper, participating in Christian fellowship, fasting or abstinence; and in *works of mercy* – doing all the good we can for the physical and spiritual needs of whomever God should bring our way: family, friends, neighbours, strangers and enemies. It is a diligent witness to the truth of our faith in whatever circumstances we may be found: at home, in the workplace, or at church. These good works flow from the fullness of our communion with God and, as such, become the means of grace by which that fullness is sustained in our hearts, extended through our lives, and returned to God in joyful prayer and thankful praise.

A vision worth striving for together

Interestingly, it was not Wesley's account of 'perfection' that caused the most controversy, but his claim that it was actually attainable in this life, and that all real Christians should agonise for it. From the moment of new birth, we are to strive continually for a gradual growth in grace, with the expectant hope that God will finally root out the sin that remains, in a moment of perfecting love. The distinguishing mark of a Methodist, however, was not the *attaining* of perfection but the *striving* after it and the way of disciplined discipleship which it called forth (cf. Eph. 4:13). This took shape in what Wesley called the 'Methodist plan', or a whole 'spiritual economy' of practices that were capable of leading persons from the initial experience of evangelical conversion and on to perfection in love. The formation of this 'plan', however, was not the result of some strategic exercise aimed at developing the spiritual 'machinery' needed to produce mature disciples. Rather, the practices that were to characterise the Methodist movement arose over time, inspired by the practical wisdom of its members and the influence of others they encountered along the way.

The Pietists of the holy living tradition inspired Wesley and a few others to form the Holy Club as a means for pursuing their emerging vision of holiness in heart and life, by 'provoking one another' to love and good works. Later, through his contact with the Moravians, Wesley came to see that this pursuit of holy living must be founded upon the evangelical experience of forgiveness and new birth. His evangelistic preaching consequently invited people into *a new personal relationship* with God through faith in the merits of Christ (i.e. justification), *a new freedom* from the tyranny of sin through the power of the Spirit (i.e. sanctification), and *a new possibility* of being perfected in love. The challenge of evangelistic preaching and Christian witness, therefore, was not to make a lone decision for Christ, but to join a community that was capable of making real Christian disciples.

Those who responded to this message of salvation and holy living were joined together into societies, with new ones planted if necessary, in order that they might pray together, receive the word of exhortation (cf. Heb. 13:22), watch over one another in love (cf. Eph. 6:18) and help each other to work out their salvation (Phil. 2:12). The only condition for membership in a Methodist society was the desire to 'flee from the wrath to come' (Mt. 3:7; cf. 1 Thess. 1:10): in other words, to forsake sin and seek the Gospel of salvation. This was not merely the evangelical experience of sins forgiven, but the 'full salvation' of sinful desires rooted out in the experience of perfect love, the possibility of a life fully devoted to God and neighbour.

Methodist societies were originally subdivided into 'classes' of twelve people as an economic expedient for raising money to cover building repairs. As class leaders went from house to house making their collections, however, they discovered a great need for spiritual guidance among the members. Eventually, these classes were gathered together as small groups, in order to hold one another accountable for seeking salvation through works of repentance and faith. Mutual accountability proceeded according to the three 'General Rules' of (1) doing no harm, (2) doing all the good one can (works of mercy), and (3) attending to the ordinances of God (works of piety). Through this means, the end of watching over one another in love was also accomplished by providing a class leader with the opportunity to advise, reprove, comfort or exhort, as the occasion required (cf. 2 Tim. 4:2). Indeed, it often took as long as two years of participation in a weekly class meeting before seekers claimed the experience of evangelical conversion.

Those 'brought to the new birth' were incorporated into 'bands' of eight to ten people, arranged by age and sex, to provide a means of 'closer union' in which they could 'confess their faults to one another, and pray for one another, that they may be healed' (cf. Jas. 5:16). This was accomplished through accountability to the same General Rules as the classes, but a more open and penetrating discourse was aimed at assisting one another grow in grace through the most besetting temptations. The bands were later diversified further to include 'penitential' bands for those who had temporarily lost sight of God, and 'select' bands for those desiring to 'press after perfection'. Wesley expected the select bands to provide 'a pattern of love, of holiness, and of all good works' (cf. 2 Tim. 3:17), imitable by members of the whole society as examples of 'whole-life discipleship'.

A vision which challenges our predispositions

I suggest that Wesley can best serve our churches and leaders as a spiritual mentor who challenges our predispositions, rather than a guru who provides us with fixed principles or guaranteed techniques for church growth. He teaches us that what the church lacks today is a vision of the end for which we strive, a vision which can call forth a whole way of life, a vision capable of inspiring the development of disciple-making practices, a vision worth staking our lives and futures upon. As a spiritual mentor, he asks us what kind of people we are called to be (or become), and what kind of community is capable of raising people like that. He reminds us that the answer to both questions can be found in the Scriptures, and that this process of discovery will involve a commitment to the long-haul adventure of costly discipleship.

Wesley calls into question our desire for off-the-shelf solutions to ministry needs, especially those technological approaches to church leadership and disciple-making that make gurus out of 'successful' pastors. Often concealed behind the visible success of churches we admire are stories of modest beginnings and endurance through real struggles to pursue a vision of authentic Christian discipleship. But the human impulse is often to subvert this wisdom into a set of simple transferable principles. Then, church marketers can merchandise those general principles as universal techniques, with all the supporting paraphernalia for applying them in different settings. Finally, we buy in to these packages, hoping to have procured the secrets of successful leadership and the keys to revitalising church life, if only we can make them work at home.

We must not turn to Wesley for general principles or universal techniques that might be procured as a technological fix to contemporary problems. Rather, we should let the history of early Methodism remind us of what is often most important about other fruitful churches and movements, namely the virtue of leadership and the vitality of Christian community that arises only through the vagaries of striving for spiritual maturity amidst the challenges of daily life. So, in conclusion, let me suggest four pieces of spiritual advice that Wesley might offer church leaders today.

First, *immerse yourselves in the Scriptures*, the biographies of saintly leaders throughout church history, and the theological vision that nurtured and sustained them. To this end, Wesley collected and edited his own Christian Library for the Methodists. What matters is not that we merely learn these things, but that we are genuinely enthused with a compelling vision for the fullness of Christian life[1] and a willingness to pursue it whatever the cost. The early Methodists read about it in tracts, heard it preached in sermons, sang about it in hymns, and wrestled for it in prayer. Find other communities that are enthused about the Christian life and hang around, as Wesley did, until you have caught some of that same enthusiasm, and been inspired with a vision for the possibility of something like it in your own church.

Second, *cultivate an adventurous spirit*, because what it actually means for you and your church to learn and live such a vision cannot be known in advance of the journey; and the practices needed to attain it cannot be pinned down by strategic planning. Seeking to live the Gospel in daily life, personally and as a community, is too complex and unpredictable for that. As an adventurer, the most enthusiastic thing one can do is set off in the company of friends, ready for the works of piety and mercy, trusting that the Spirit will provide the practical wisdom needed to address tactical issues along the way.

Third, *consider the use of disciplined Christian fellowship,* where members can hold each other accountable for striving to become mature disciples. As with the early Methodists, and many other renewal movements throughout church history, it is likely that such adventurous company will be found in the form of small-group fellowship, where the scriptural practices of Christian discipleship naturally flourish. What is more, the natural environment for apprenticeship in the art of sharing our faith is the context of Christian fellowship itself. As we learn how to give testimony to one another about the saving work of God in and through the struggles of everyday life, we also learn a skill that is capable of relating the Gospel to the ordinary experience of all those with whom we share our lives.

Fourth, *anticipate trouble among the troops,* because the kind of mutual dependency, intimacy and accountability required to sustain an adventure of this sort is likely to raise painful disagreement about both the means and the end. The truth is, we find ourselves holding out for a common vision and a common life among those who have been predisposed by the dominant culture to define their own private ends and choose their own personal means of accomplishing them. Struggling to discern and strive for a common vision and a common life, however, actually constitutes the very essence of our adventure; forbearing one another in love is our witness to the truth about God in an unbelieving world (Jn. 13:34-35; 17:20-21; Eph. 4:2; Col. 3:13).

♦ ♦ ♦ ♦

Further reading

Henderson, D. Michael, *John Wesley's Class Meeting: A Model for Making Disciples* (Evangel Publishing House, 1998)

Manskar, Steven, *A Perfect Love* (Discipleship Resources, 2003)

Meadows, Philip, 'Embodying Conversion' in Kenneth Collins and John Tyson (eds.), *Conversion in the Wesleyan Tradition* (Abingdon Press, 2001)

Wesley, John, 'The Character of a Methodist' in Rupert Davies (ed.), *The Works of John Wesley*, Volume 9 (Abingdon Press, 1990)

Notes

1 I take 'enthusiasm' in the positive sense that Wesley did, even in the Age of Reason, to mean being literally filled with God!

6

Shaping the disciple's mind

Graham McFarlane

Graham is Senior Lecturer in Systematic Theology at London School of Theology and lectures in a discipline that seeks both to show and teach the internal coherence and consistency of each doctrine in itself and in relation to other aspects of Christian thought. He trained at London School of Theology (BA and MA), taught RE for four years and worked for L'Abri Fellowship. He took his PhD at King's College under the late Colin Gunton. His publications include Why do you believe what you believe about Jesus?

We live in times of unprecedented change and therefore incredible opportunity. The good news for the early twenty-first century is that for the first time in its modern history the church has been liberated from the dualisms which have bound it. Abstract theology is no longer viable – it has to work! In this chapter Graham explores the pastoral function of doctrine – of thinking Christianly – in shaping the motivations, desires and ultimately the priorities and behaviour of a follower of Jesus today.

For reflection

- How much energy and resource do we put into thinking Christianly about life in today's world?
- What might it mean to 'do theology' as described in this chapter in our church communities?

Shaping the disciple's mind

One of the most exciting things about studying theology today, and trying to be doctrinally relevant where it matters, is the fact that this is a time of unprecedented change. For the more forward-thinking, such change brings incredible opportunity. We are poised on the cusp of a completely new era – something that only happens within western culture every five hundred or thousand years. It would be wrong to see what is happening as a revolution. But it is clear that we are experiencing a significant paradigm shift in the values and orientation points of our culture, profound changes in our worldview. Not being a fashion victim, I am loath to describe this as postmodernity. Indeed I think it is fairer to say that for most people in the UK modernity is still very much alive and kicking. Therefore, let's describe the present context as more one of late – or even better, 'knackered' – modernity. It is more a case of our culture displaying the natural outworking of modernity.[1] For the student and practitioner of theology, however, our fundamental questions remain the same: How does our culture manifest itself? How should the body of Christ respond?

How does our culture manifest itself?

This first question concerns the big picture. It's about understanding the world in which we live. It behoves the student of theology to be aware of the present context of cultural upheaval simply because this is the context in which their belief and practice will have to operate. I get a real buzz when I pick up *The Times* and read social commentators saying, 'There's an absence in our culture that not even New Labour's ersatz vision of modernity can fill.'[2] Of course, this 'absence' has been well researched. Sociologist Tony Walter highlights this societal trend that undergirds our whole modernist/ postmodernist economy that is based on consumerism.[3] In the contemporary western context everything has a price.

Until recently, we have had to rely on the first wave of 'church' change from American theologians such as Stanley Hauerwas, William Willimon and Robert Jenson as they unpack what this militant consumerism means for the church. Of late, however, David Ford has helpfully expressed this epoch in terms of 'overwhelmings'.[4] That is, a strange thing happens with the demise of any universally accepted framework for assessing information and the knowledge we have. Rather than not having enough information, we end up by having too much, since there are no criteria for filtering out the necessary from the unnecessary. Lack of a universal truth grid leads to a demand for more information that we hope will somehow help us to deal with this sense of being overwhelmed.

How should the body of Christ respond?

This second question concerns the church. It's about the need to skilfully audit and then address the ecclesial pathologies in the light of this wider culture. It's about looking at whether the way we 'do church' within our different church expressions is really helping Christians exercise their belief and practice in the contexts in which they live. The cultural context described briefly above has had devastating effects on the internal reality of the church. During the era of modernity, the church has moved from operating with a coherent set of rules and markers to operating on the basis of either theological anarchy or theological complacency. So we note that at the genesis of modernity, teaching was a significant element of church initiation whereby the convert was inducted over a period of up to three years in the grammar of the faith.[5] Now, however, such catechism has been whittled down to the ubiquitous Alpha (if one is lucky).

Our uncertainty about what to believe manifests itself, ultimately, in the kind of church communities we spawn. At the twilight of the Enlightenment project, it would appear that the church that cuts itself off from its historical tradition cuts itself off from being able to change and survive robustly. Why? Because this leads to an ahistorical and spiritually subjective faith which then falls into the trap of dumbing-down its message in order to accommodate to the surrounding culture. Not a particularly helpful context within which to shape the minds of Jesus' disciples. What happens is that the priorities necessary for producing behaviour appropriate to those who belong to God's kingdom are inevitably watered down. Instead they are heavily influenced by the world, or even by 'religion'.

Needless to say, these are not new phenomena to hit the church. Rather, they appear to be temptations that lie at the heart of all attempts at living out the Judaeo-Christian faith. From the Jewish Scriptures comes the exhortation:

> Remember the days of old,
> consider the years long past;
> ask your father, and he will inform you;
> your elders, and they will tell you (Deut. 32:7).

These words are picked up in the Christian Scriptures in the encouragement to Jude to 'contend for the faith that was once for all entrusted to the saints' (Jude 3).

Therefore there appear to be two imperatives that lie at the heart of discipleship. First, there is the need to engage with both the world of faith and the world within which that faith will be practised. Secondly, there is the need to do so through the use of one's mind – its will, its affections and its reasoning.

The task ahead

We can see that the contemporary scene is one of change. But in what way is it also one of opportunity? First of all, it goes without saying that at moments of upheaval and crisis what was once established can be disestablished. This is seen quite clearly in the way the discipline of Christian doctrine, or what we might more loosely call Christian theology, has been perceived in the recent past and yet how that perception is changing today.

The relationship between theology and modernity has never been a stable one. In terms of shaping disciples' minds and its practical outworking in pastoral application, modern theology has had a very uneasy relationship with grass-roots Christian discipleship. It has facilitated a divorce between text and context, between text and interpretation, between text and practice, all of which have been seriously debilitating to any vigorous discipleship. In the end, small wonder that so many Christians deem the need for a theologically robust mind and heart as irrelevant, or as something required only by the erudite or academic.

However, this could not be further from the truth, as the biblical texts above have shown. Perhaps, just perhaps, the existence of a weak church, of disillusioned disciples, of flabby Christianity, can be traced back to the rise of contentless and shallow minds on the part of those who follow Jesus. After all, Scripture is replete with admonitions concerning the content of our minds.

> Keep your heart (mind) with all vigilance, for from it flow the springs of life (Prov. 4:23).

> We take every thought captive to obey Christ (2 Cor. 10:5).

There is therefore an exciting opportunity, at a moment of change, for disciples of Jesus to undo the impasse that has grown between who one is and what one believes. Such a division is simply unbiblical, let alone something that defies all current cognitive and behavioural psychologies.

The good news for the early twenty-first century is that for the first time in its modern history, the church has been liberated from the dualisms that have bound it. Rather, the proper role of Christian theology, including its role in forming disciples' minds and hearts, is beginning to re-emerge. Why is that? Because it was not just the Berlin Wall that came down in the late 1980s. It was also the beginning of the demise of a theological mindset that had prevailed for more than two hundred years. No longer was it viable to develop an abstract theology. Rather – and this is the good point about today – in a consumerist culture it had to work.

Thus the task of thinking Christianly, of holding to correct doctrine, will be commensurate with the traditions and history of the church, from the early church through to today. In opposition to all postmodern tendencies, the disciple of Jesus proclaims that there is a story that holds centre stage. The new imperative is to find ways in which the faith can be translated into the diverse contexts in which each one of us finds ourselves. After all, isn't that the drive that has brought you to read this book? Isn't this what lies behind the tortuous routes we all take in order to make Christ known? Isn't it the desire to make one's personal relationship with Jesus Christ and the God and Father of our Lord Jesus Christ relevant to our neighbours? And that requires hard graft.

What is the nature of the task?

Perhaps we can answer this question in two ways. Firstly, there is the descriptive element. That is, how do we describe the task of 'doing theology'? To put it in a nutshell, theology

1. Provides a basis upon which Christian discipleship is practised (doctrine)
2. Facilitates skills that are life-enhancing (ethics)
3. Feeds a life of worship (lifestyle)

But on top of this is the prescriptive dimension. That is, just how do we go about this? Now, this is where the window of opportunity occurs. A space has arisen within our culture, a space that will remain open only for a short while. It is what we do during the emergence of this space that will determine the shape of Christian thinking within our culture for decades to come. And what are we doing?

We are experiencing a historic shift from rational theology that is divorced from context and praxis to what might be called a more earthed and holistic, or convergent, theology that recognises the need for what we believe and teach to be exercised. That is, theology that actually scratches where the itch is. There are different titles for this discipline, the most helpful contemporary one being that offered by Ellen Charry as 'sapiential theology'.[6] Sapiential theology is a theology that is not only for the clergy but also for the laity, one that works at grass-roots level and engenders a life of worship and creative growth. It is an understanding of the place of doctrine, of what we believe, as not simply an ivory tower phenomenon but something in which every disciple of Jesus must engage – or not, to their peril.

In business community terms, it involves the acquisition of certain 'transferable skills'. Being a disciple of Jesus whose motivation, desires and, ultimately, priorities and behaviour reflect being mentored by Jesus Christ does not come *au naturel*, but is very much something that requires discipline, time, energy, commitment, and the sacrifice of the 'goodies' for the better things of God's kingdom. It requires, therefore, the ability

- to identify the questions and needs of the church and the world around
- to identify with the Christian Gospel and traditions
- to develop answers that converge with the need
- to release people into service and worship.

Moving towards the Christological centre

Let me declare my colours here. I am no fan of the kind of Christian thinking that demands an excellent memory but little application. Rather, my theology converges on an understanding of, and relationship with, the risen

Jesus Christ that demands engagement with the world at the places where it does not work, where people are not attractive. It is a perception of the world that makes no sense without firm doctrinal reasons. And it is this way of believing that has fed and harvested the kind of theology that has been practised at grass-roots level since the days of Pentecost.

Jesus himself anticipates it when he asks his disciples, 'Who do you say that I am?' And he elicits profoundly doctrinal answers. The content of the New Testament did not fall out of the sky: it was the product of intense and prolonged theological reflection and practice. Sure, the early Christians worshipped Jesus long before they understood who he was. But that did not keep them from the imperative to study, to work, to show themselves men and women who could rightly handle the word of God, and to pass on to the next generation a way of Christian living that was both rigorous in its content and radical in its outworking. Thus there has to be living faith, one that moves away from the attitude which says, 'Just gimme the facts!' In other words, the kind of doctrine that shapes disciples' minds is one that first and foremost describes who God is, what Jesus has done for us, how the Spirit transforms, who the people of God are. It's not the kind of doctrine that merely ends in prescriptive behaviour or a rigid framework for the Christian life. Instead, it connects radical and holy living with the very nature and purposes of God. It's a doctrine that shapes a relationship with him and so opens up the possibility of a dynamic discipleship that actually works.

This demands, then, an engagement with the world of Jesus in order that we might, in turn, engage with our own. To some extent, evangelical theologies have been trying to do this since their birth. So it is affirming, in a sense, to see in recent times theologians of the stature of

Hans Frei or George Lindbeck argue for a return to the world of the New Testament and let it speak to us. To that extent we need to rediscover this world and engage with it.

Pointing forward

Ellen Charry helpfully points out that today Christian doctrine lives on the margins of the secular culture. As Christian thinkers we have lost the high ground. Perhaps this is a good thing. We now have to sing for our supper rather than assume it will be waiting for us. And of course, unless we sing well, we won't get fed! However, this marginalisation has come with a tremendous cost. We are, as Charry forcefully reminds us, 'moral and intellectual barbarians'.[7] How did this happen? Because our forefathers allowed the disciplines of theology and spirituality, of doctrine and ethics, of belief and lifestyle, to be separated.

Ultimately, we reap what we have sown. Thus today we inhabit a church culture that is almost entirely illiterate concerning its history, tradition and identity. Sociologists may map the decline; psychologists may identify possible malignancies; economists may tender solutions. But it is only from the arena of thinking faith, from biblically and theologically minded practitioners, that the art of theological imagination can emerge – something that, when taken up by the life of God, can transform the communities you serve and lead.

This is the high calling of thinking Christianly, of pursuing proper Christian doctrine, of engaging with the task of theology proper. It demands an understanding that doctrine without application – theology without ethics – is ultimately sterile. In the end, it means that what we believe must engage not only with mind – rigorously so – but also with personality, with spirit. Perhaps we can put it another way. The imperative between doctrine and ethics is this: doctrines aim to be good for us by reforming our character.

This will, in the end, involve us in some work that is groundbreaking and challenging as well as exciting and demanding. It also means, as Tom Oden so clearly warns us, that, 'The church that weds itself to modernity is already a widow within postmodernity.'[8] And we shall not avoid such judgement without serious engagement with our minds and our wills. For that to happen we require visceral and penetrating doctrine to challenge the status quo to which every western believer is attracted, whether it be in the world – do we become like Demas?[9] – or of religion – do we become postmodern Pharisees?

♦ ♦ ♦ ♦

Further reading

Charry, Ellen T., *By the Renewing of Your Minds* (Oxford University Press, 1997)

Ford, David, *Theology: A Very Short Introduction* (Oxford University Press, 2000)

Lakeland, Paul, *Postmodernity: Christian Identity in a Fragmented Age* (Fortress Press, 1997)

Oden, Thomas C., *Requiem: A Lament in Three Movements* (Abingdon Press, 1995)

Clark, David K., *To Know and Love God* (Crossway, 2003)

Notes

1 Fredric Jameson, 'Postmodernism, or, The Cultural Logic of Late Capitalism', cited in Paul Lakeland, *Postmodernity: Christian Identity in a Fragmented Age* (Fortress Press, 1997).

2 Jason Cowley, *The Times*, 28 February 2000.

3 Tony Walter, *All You Love is Need* (SPCK, 1985) published in the USA as *Need: the New Religion*.

4 David Ford, *Theology: A Very Short Introduction* (Oxford University Press, 2000).

5 See also chapter 4: From darkness to light.

6 See Ellen Charry, *By the Renewing of Your Minds* (Oxford University Press, 1997).

7 Ibid.

8 Thomas C. Oden, *Requiem: A Lament in Three Movements* (Abingdon Press, 1995).

9 2 Tim. 4:10.

Pastoral perspectives

7

Why do churches resist disciple-making?

Steve Davie

Following a career in local government, Steve Davie spent twelve years representing The Navigators in Scotland and the South of England, and for the last thirteen years has been a church minister. He has completed a PhD on the recent history of evangelical ecclesiology and is currently team rector at St Bartholomew's Horley.

It's not hard to get people to agree that disciple-making is crucial to the growth of Christians and their church. But it's rare to find a church where whole-life disciple-making is core to their culture, where it shapes everything they do. There are dynamics at work that resist disciple-making. In this chapter, Steve reflects on his experiences in order to understand why.

For reflection

- Where are the main areas of resistance to disciple-making in your situation?
- Is there someone you could encourage for a time on their journey as a disciple of Christ?

Why do churches resist disciple-making?

Do you remember the 1970s book *Hudson Taylor's Spiritual Secret*? I guess some Christians wanted to know the 'secret', a higher spiritual plane or process that would draw them into God's real plan through a door that many had missed. Disciple-making is neither a panacea nor a method. Rather, I understand disciple-making to be a vision, a heartbeat, an emphasis, a process – a longing to see men and women not only become Christians but grow in Christ and reach others. It is the Christ-centred, Spirit-filled desire to see others contribute to the Great Commission in their own context, their workplace, family or church. Disciple-making can be developed within all spiritualities and in every culture in which the local church ministers. While gifting, character and perspective are essential marks of spiritual maturity, so is the heart and practical ability to help others come to Christ and grow. However, I find that churches resist disciple-making. Why is that?

The faith to become disciple-makers

Most Christians have not been personally discipled, nor have they discipled others, and it can be hard to believe God for something we have not experienced. However, that need not be so. 'Daws' Trotman, founder of The Navigators, led the counsellor training for the 1954-5 Billy Graham missions in London and Glasgow. Some 4.5 million people heard the Gospel message, and ninety thousand who responded were invited to come to the front of the meeting to hear a more detailed explanation of how to invite Jesus to be their Lord and Saviour. Each was counselled and prayed with, and their names were passed to churches in their area: 'follow-up' entered the vocabulary of the churches. So much is history.[1]

But the story has not yet been told of those who trained the counsellors and began a disciple-making ministry in Britain. Shortly before his death in an accident in 1956, Daws spoke to a staff gathering with a message that is very relevant to our situation.

> Let me tell you what I believe the need of the hour is. . . . *I believe it is an army of soldiers, dedicated to Jesus Christ, who believe not only that he is God, but that he can fulfil every promise he has ever made, and that there isn't anything too hard for him.* . . . I believe with all my heart that the reason so many wonderful Christians don't accomplish more in their lives is that they don't believe Jesus meant what He said. . . . The last thing He said was 'All power is given unto me. I'm giving you your orders now. Go and teach all nations and see that every created being hears the Word'. . . . How did that message go? Not by telephone, not by television, but by tell-a-person . . . everyone had someone else to tell. . . . Maybe the greatest problem today is that we try to put into printed form that which should go from lip to ear and heart to heart. The need of the hour, as far as I am concerned, is to believe that God is God and that He is a lot more interested in getting the job done than you or I.[2]

I asked two friends of mine why churches resist disciple-making. Their response was immediate: 'It's hard!' However, if Daws was right, the hardest thing is to trust God. So this is where we must start.

Jane is a good friend of ours who has gathered a couple of other young mothers to read the Bible and pray together each week. One woman found personal faith after a painful divorce, is now happily married and speaks about how her faith affects the way she treats the children where she works. Another mother was confirmed some years ago but still finds believing God difficult. A further woman has recently moved into the area and joined them. Of course, conversation often turns to how difficult their traditional church is, but under Jane's gentle guidance, they continue to support the church, to teach the children from the Bible, to apply God's word to their own challenging situations, and together they make visits to other more vibrant churches. Be in no doubt, Jane is disciple-making. She has faith that God will use her to help others grow in faith and in living more fully as a Christian in today's world. Jane is the most important part of the disciple-making ministry and its basic form.

We need to find ways to encourage the Janes, to resource them, team them up with others in their area and enable them to see that what they are doing is very valuable in God's kingdom. And that applies to many ministers who may be disciple-making in unsympathetic or apathetic churches. However, Jane's is not a disciple-making church, largely because most of the members don't really believe God calls them to be disciple-makers. The resources, time and energy of the church are therefore directed elsewhere – mainly towards keeping their show on the road.

The power of the lowest common denominator

Many other churches, however, readily aspire to see God's kingdom come in their neighbourhood. They attempt to have lively worship on Sunday; the minister and the lay preachers try to be both Bible-based and practical in their teaching; they encourage the house group leaders; they tithe and have committed pastoral visitors; they may have tried Alpha with some success. The key to this church is Christian fellowship and the central messages are the love of God for the sinner, the call to repentance, and encouragement for those who are tempted to fall away from their discipleship. However, this is not a disciple-making church.

Why does it resist disciple-making? After all, there are several faithful 'Janes' here. But others say, 'Let's not go too far!' It would not be right for the house group leaders or the minister to show any kind of favouritism to particular people in the church, as it might leave out others – and some are quite sensitive. Some members have come out of 'heavy-shepherding' churches from the 1970s. Other members have been offended by the way they were asked to move on from running the Lunch Club, the way their difficult child was spoken to in Sunday Club, or the fact that when they were struggling a bit, no one seemed to notice for weeks that they were not in church. So of course this church believes in making disciples and in spiritual growth, but only so long as the peace is not disturbed. In fact, this is a lowest common denominator church, organised on the basis of keeping everyone on board, minimising complaints and conflicts. In effect, this church is led by those who might complain.

Accommodated but not strengthened

One day I had to replace a rotten fence at the bottom of our garden. I set in concrete the metal supports for the wooden uprights, and fixed the fence panels, but when the wind blew, the fence fell down because the soil was too soft and the concrete not deep enough. I had to halve the height of the fence to suit the soil. When Paul revisited the churches in Lystra, Iconium and Antioch, he *strengthened* the disciples. When he did a circuit of the churches in Syria and southern Turkey, he set out to *strengthen* the churches. When he sent Timothy back to Thessalonica, Timothy's job was to *establish* and exhort them in their faith.[3] The word used for *strengthen* and *establish* means to fix, to make fast, to set. It was a work done by Paul and Timothy under God. We know that they took account of the soil conditions. If our ministry is based on avoiding trouble, our house group leaders and our minister will be worn out and the choir mistress will have turned into a virago to survive – all because our new disciples for years past have not been *strengthened,* they have been *accommodated*. They have certainly become Christians, they are born again, but they are not strong in their faith and they will fall over when the wind blows. They have not been taught how to grow.

Furthermore, when Paul wrote to some of the Christians in areas he had visited on those trips, he reminded them that the job of the apostles, prophets, evangelists, pastors and teachers ministering in their gifts was to equip the saints for the work of ministry.[4] If our vision is to establish people in the faith and to equip the saints, we will not be focused on keeping everyone on board, nor will our church members be weary of being told what to do – someone will be walking with them to show them how to live.

Many churches realise this and run courses for potential leaders. Wise churches realise that the issue is not just the constant demand for new leadership but also the need for those who could be valuable 'number twos', those who might be gifted administrators or have a social conscience and want to serve as school governors or get into local politics. Their need is Christian maturity, for someone to show them how to be everyday disciples and how to help others become disciples, not just tell them to do it. One of the easiest ways is to run courses such as Alpha or Christianity Explored for those becoming Christians, then Emmaus or 2:7 or one of several other courses available for those needing to grow or for emerging leadership.[5]

But courses are not a comprehensive answer. Becoming a disciple-making church means changing some of the default settings of the church. Church culture is often oriented around weekend and evening activity rather than whole-life Christianity. Churches have a tendency to lock in to the local neighbourhood and pay little attention to the places where their members are living and working throughout the week. And the church often presents spiritual growth as somehow divorced from life in the real world. These limited perspectives shape our approach to disciple-making.

Limited perspectives

If your church believes God's promises and is determined to see Christians grow, what else could prevent it from being an effective disciple-making church? A predetermined, powerful, but limited theology. Several years ago I was asked to set up visits to ministers of two large, city-centre churches with whom I had good contacts. I was trying to start 2:7, a comprehensive programme designed to help churches with disciple-making.[6] Both churches understood preaching to be the primary vehicle for evangelism and Christian growth, and both ministers agreed to give me some time. One minister was happy to allow this new programme as an experiment, but the second cancelled the appointment because he was too busy. The meeting never materialised, largely because the church was overwhelmingly confident that preaching was all that was required to win and mature Christians.

The same approach might well exist in a very charismatic church, with a theology that relates purely to the prophetic. It's not that either preaching or the prophetic is right or wrong, but Christians learn in a variety of ways.[7] If a church determines that only one way of learning is permitted, it will have a ministry to a limited kind of person. It might be very successful at that, but its disciple-making potential will be limited.

Jesus said that we should love the Lord with all our heart, soul, mind and strength.[8] The danger of relying on one method of teaching or learning is that followers of Jesus become very skilled at that one method of intake. While heart people learn mainly through experience, and mind people mainly through books or talks, soul people tend to be pragmatic, and hands-on people learn through doing. Of course most of us are comfortable with one means of perception, but we need our other means to be developed. This is particularly true if we want to mature new leaders who can minister to a variety of personalities and into the variety of cultures within our society.

What is true of our style of learning is also true of our preferred means of intake: some love a large meeting, others only flourish in a small group. However, we become rounded disciples if we can learn the benefits of learning and teaching in the large group, the small group and one-to-one mentoring. Many large churches excel in large and small groups, but the mentoring is often ignored. This is a pity, for it is here that personal care, application, accountability and learning reach their target. Jesus understood this. He preached to crowds and encouraged or challenged the small group of disciples, but was able to give very specific input to individuals.

Adopting these methods as part of an intentional disciple-making strategy will grow a variety of disciples in a whole range of situations. This is important in any size of church, whatever its spirituality.

But limited perspectives can also apply to other areas of our theology. Our understanding of who God is, who we are as human beings, our identity in Christ, our grasp of the comprehensive scope of God's salvation and of his plans and purposes for humanity and for the created world – all these will shape our picture of what a disciple of Christ looks like. Churches can be ineffective in their disciple-making because they have a limited perspective on what it means to be a 'whole-life' disciple-making community.

Focused, but missing the target?

This is the hardest part of disciple-making: you know that you want to see mature disciples among your young people, in the family life stage and in the third age, the active retired. You know that ministering to young professionals is different from ministering to those with manual jobs. Your heart is to grow disciples among them all, but it just doesn't seem to happen. The new word on the block is 'intentional' disciple-making.[9] The concept is the same difficult one as has always existed: under God, you get what you aim for, and if you aim for nothing, that's what you get.

The key to multiplying disciples is to aim for a few, high-quality relationships. Jesus taught crowds, but he ministered deeply to the twelve and, some would argue, he invested even more in Peter, James and John. Paul planted churches, preached to crowds and formed travelling teams. But he seemed to have a special place for Timothy, and we have two letters written to this young pastor. The advice he gave to his protégé was to find FAT people to invest in: Faithful, Available and Teachable. Paul wrote, 'What you have heard from me through many witnesses entrust to faithful people who will be able to teach others as well.'[10] It was vital for Timothy to pick very carefully those who were already *faithful* with the resources they had; those who were *available* to teach others, whether individually or in groups; and those who were *teachable*. There are four spiritual generations in this verse, and Paul would finish his disciple-making job when he saw the fourth generation. But he would only see the fourth generation if Timothy invested in FAT people.

Much of my problem is that I want to help everyone who seems to want to learn. What I need to do is to find those who really want to learn: who are prepared to pay the price of focusing their efforts, of learning the deep character lessons required for maturing in Christ and helping others to grow. Then I need to start them teaching others. Always train the next generation to teach others.

Conclusion

Why do churches resist disciple-making? Because we don't believe that God wants us to be disciple-makers; because we are satisfied to see Christians learn merely to survive rather than truly grow; because we want to please many people in our churches; because our limited theologies describe too narrow a picture of what we're aiming for; and because we are not intentional in our disciple-making. To turn these factors around needs a change of perspective, a change of prayer and a change of purpose.

Hannah prayed, 'O Lord of Hosts, if only you will look on the misery of your servant, and remember me, and not forget your servant, but will give to your servant a male child . . .'[11] Hannah desired a physical son, but it was clear that Samuel was also a spiritual son. The apostle Paul also spoke of the need for spiritual children,[12] and whatever our circumstances or spirituality it is very possible for each of us to have father/son or mother/daughter relationships in the Lord, relationships that will reproduce.

It matters that churches are resistant to disciple-making. But it also matters whether you and I are listening to what God wants us to do and to be. The truth is, he wants me to be concerned about the things I can influence, such as my heart and mind devotion to his love and glory, the quality of my teaching and learning, and the choice of those in whom I am to invest my life (not merely those with whom I am to spend my time). In short, I need to have an intentional disciple-making ministry. I can do that with one or two individuals, and as a church leader I can structure the church groups to that end, investing in FAT leaders and workers who are going to make that significant difference in the lives of others. I need to model what I'm passionate about. It might not be the full story on disciple-making, but it can certainly move us towards becoming a disciple-making community while we start to tackle the very real areas of resistance within our churches that I've described.

♦ ♦ ♦ ♦

Further reading

Collinson, Sylvia Wilkey, *The Significance of Jesus' Educational Methods for Today's Church* (Paternoster, 2004)

Graham, Billy, *Just As I Am* (HarperCollins, 1997)

Skinner, B., *With Integrity of Heart and with Skilful Hand* (NavPress, 1998)

Wright, Walter C., *Mentoring: The Promise of Relational Leadership* (Paternoster, 2004)

Notes

1 See, for example, Frank Colquhoun, *Harringay Story* (Hodder & Stoughton, 1955), William Martin, *A Prophet with Honour: the Billy Graham Story* (Hutchinson, 1992) for an excellent account of the Harringay Crusade, and Billy Graham, *Just As I Am* (HarperCollins, 1997).

2 Dawson E. Trotman, *Great is Thy Faithfulness* (The Navigators, 1957). See also Betty Skinner, *Daws: A Man who Trusted God* (Zondervan, 1974).

3 Acts 14:22; 15:41; 1 Thess. 3:2.

4 Eph. 4:11-12. See also chapter 3: Ephesians 4 ministries and spiritual formation, and chapter 9: What are leaders for?

5 See www.alphacourse.org; www.christianityexplored.com; or www.licc.org.uk/imagine/resources/courses for reviews of some of the main courses available.

6 http://navigators.co.uk/church/2-7-info.php

7 See chapter 13 on adult learning and chapter 14 on this subject from an emerging church perspective.

8 Mk. 12:30.

9 See chapter 16: Experiments in twenty-first-century disciple-making.

10 2 Tim. 2:2.

11 1 Sam. 1:11.

12 See, for example, 1 Cor. 4:14-16.

8

Empire or kingdom: the pastor's dilemma

John S. Smith

John grew up in Liverpool, studied ecological science, and pursued a career as a town planner in Scottish local government for eleven years. He served as a pastor in Scottish Baptist churches for sixteen years. From 1999 to 2006 John was UK Director of the Evangelical Alliance, committed to a movement for change in our churches and in our nation today. John has recently become senior pastor of Milton Baptist Church, Weston-super-Mare, where he continues to pursue his passion of turning the church inside out to turn the world upside down.

Local church leaders are naturally passionate about helping their churches to become places where they do what they do well. Though building the local church is commonly motivated by an evangelistic vision, it often has the effect of using the time, energy and resources of its members to run the church's activities and 'keep the show on the road'. Writing from hard-won experience, John explores the mindset needed to release people into whole-life discipleship.

For reflection

- In what ways do you experience the kingdom / church dilemma?
- How does it impact whole-life disciple-making in your church?

Empire or kingdom: the pastor's dilemma

Local church leaders often feel an overwhelming passion, vision, or even obligation to build the local church in order to ensure it functions excellently. This internal focus, although commonly motivated evangelistically, usually has the effect of sucking active members into serving as a volunteer workforce that runs the activities of the local church. Involvement in Christian service through para-church agencies, in the wider geographical area or in workplace Christian groupings, may be viewed as a conflict of loyalties. This may be exacerbated further by involvement of members in social or political activities that are apparently not at all related to the church's mission.

There is evidence that a new vision of church is attractive to, and is easily caught by, many pastors who view Ephesians 4:11 not simply in relation to works of service in the local church, but to works of service wherever God calls. They recognise the local church dispersed as well as gathered. The vision is all very well, but who will resource and run church ministries if we modify our expectations of total commitment to the local church agenda? And how, in practical terms, do pastors facilitate a process by which members feel released into the whole of life when they have not been trained in this area or their personal knowledge of the workplace is either dated or limited? How will they initiate change? Who will resource them? Is the system that pays and appraises them too rigid for such a radical expression of church? How will a pastor make the transition from building empire to advancing kingdom?

The landscape of expectations

The 'Four Spiritual Laws' of Campus Crusade for Christ founder Bill Bright began with these encouraging words: 'God loves you and has a wonderful plan for your life.' For many pastors, however, this could easily be rewritten: 'God loves you and everyone else has a wonderful plan for your life.' Almost regardless of what was discussed or negotiated in the period leading to a pastoral appointment, once someone takes up that pastoral office, they will find they are subject to a wide range of expectations. Some will be very personal:

> 'I want to be fed from the Word of God so that I can mature and develop as a Christian.'
> 'I want a positive experience of church services for myself, my children and any visitors someone else may happen to bring.'
> 'I want to see this church move to the cutting edge of innovation, in worship, in communication, in outreach strategy.'
> 'I want this church to grow in numbers and influence.'
> 'I want this church to have a high profile in the nation.'

In the midst of all of this, of course, the pastor will have personal expectations. Some will be based on what God has used in achievements elsewhere. Some will be based on what never actually got off the ground in the last church. As pastors attend conferences and read exciting stories of church growth in other locations, they may expect and long that something similar will happen where they are. Their sense of God's honour or, in some cases, their own ego may create an expectation of church growth and development that is entirely unrealistic or inappropriate given the sociological and demographic characteristics of the area.

There will be other external expectations placed on them, which will vary according to churchmanship. In centrally governed denominations they may have been selected for a particular purpose such as closing down the church or brokering a merger with a neighbouring congregation. Success may be measured in various ways – by growth in numbers attending the services, by numbers responding for believer's baptism or confirmation, by financial criteria, or by the progress of a building project.

The lessons of experience

As a pastor in Scottish Baptist churches I soon realised that my weekly routine and responsibilities were very different from those of the parish minister in the nearby Church of Scotland congregation. My Presbyterian colleagues seemed to spend their time on a weekly round of funerals, weddings and chaplaincy responsibilities. Some had more funerals in a week than I had in a year, or more weddings in a year than I had in a dozen. Did I have a light load, then? No, not at all. I poured my energy into preparing to communicate God's word: two major new sermons a week, plus a children's talk, and perhaps house group material for midweek. I couldn't quite understand how it was that others joked about the Saturday evening struggle to prepare a sermon for the next morning. I had spent the lion's share of the week getting ready.

I too was involved in the community, taking regular services in a retirement home and sharing chaplaincy work in local primary and secondary schools. But alongside this, as a church we set up a full range of what we called bridge-building ministries – for mums and toddlers, children, teenagers, ladies, senior citizens. Somehow we never quite got there with the men! Here was the philosophy: 'Let's create attractive user-friendly environments into which we can insert some kind of Gospel message.' Success would be measured when contacts became committed members of the church. This did not happen very often. But we lived in hope. The adage 'God does not call us to be successful; he calls us to be faithful' was our safety net when we did not see the longed-for progress.

The expectation I had placed upon myself was this: to do whatever it takes to grow this local church. The focus was therefore more on building up the local church than on building up individuals for discipleship wherever they spent their waking hours, or for influencing the atmosphere of the community in which we were located. Everything happened with an eye to bridge-building, with the expectation that people would cross over bridges of friendship or care into our local church life.

This philosophy had implications for our involvement in ecumenical relationships. We saw them as a diversion. It also had implications for our involvement with others in area- or city-wide evangelistic initiatives. Our goals were clear: we got involved because we wanted some of the enquirers to end up in our church. I struggled when church members chose to put their time and energy into para-church agencies rather than our own activities, especially when some of those were desperately short of staff. And of course it was even more difficult to understand the regular involvement of our members with secular charities or recreational clubs. How did they find time to be president of the darts or bowling club? How did they find time to play golf regularly or train with a football team? We had important 'spiritual' work for them to do within the context of our local church programmes.

On one occasion I received an invitation to become chaplain to the national headquarters of a public utility that was located within walking distance of our church building. As with other invitations to outside opportunities for service, I took this to the leaders of the church for consideration. The reasons for refusal were informative. 'Very few of the people who work there live in this area.' 'Some of them travel forty miles each way to get there.' 'It won't bring people to our church.' I never took up that appointment. Yet as I reflected over the years, the reasons for not considering it further appeared flawed.

We found it difficult to rejoice when we led the initiative to bring Billy Graham live-links to the south side of Glasgow. Each night, as local host, I applied Billy Graham's appeal to the local situation and people responded. But when we balanced out all the effort we had put in against the fact that not one enquirer was referred to our church, we were disappointed. In fact we decided to change our strategy for Mission Scotland when, two years later, Billy Graham himself came to town. In the event, we did not do much better.

I look back with a degree of horror to a home visit that I made to one woman who had responded at Mission Scotland and applied for baptism and church membership. I thought I was being very wise when I asked her husband, who had not been to Mission Scotland, if he was comfortable with the increased level of commitment to church activities that his wife's church membership would involve. He did not understand what I meant. He did not anticipate that her involvement as a church member would stretch past Sunday morning attendance. Not surprisingly, in the light of our expectations, she didn't stay around our church very long after she joined us.

I want to dwell for a moment on what I now see as a missed opportunity. This woman was a high-flyer in the investment world, making daily decisions involving thousands, if not millions, of pounds. Instead of figuring out how we could help her live out her discipleship on a daily basis in such an influential and pressurised environment, I had seen her as part of a volunteer workforce for church-based activities. I was building an empire instead of facilitating the growth of the kingdom.

Here is the pastor's dilemma: how do I keep this show on the road, week after week, and ensure it is a good show, an attractive show, while at the same time releasing people into the ministry to which God has called them in the whole of life? Nothing I was prioritising was wrong; it was all good stuff. It was simply focused too sharply in the wrong place. I thought my vision was broad – let's build a big church, so that we can attract and influence more and more people for Jesus – when in fact it was narrow. Gifted men and women were tied up in running the ministries of the church. Perhaps I was preventing them from serving as salt or yeast in other places where they might have greater opportunity to influence others for Christ. My question was, 'How can I reach this community for Christ through building a strong, vibrant local church?' A better, more strategic question might have been, 'How can I equip the members of this church to be influential for Jesus wherever God has placed them in society?' For change to take place I would have to prioritise kingdom over local church.

From empire to kingdom

Such a statement is ripe for misunderstanding. I believe in local church. I agree with Bill Hybels when he describes local church as the hope of the world. The dilemma is this: is running church, as we know it, the most effective way to bring hope to the world? Is such internally focused, intensive labour the best strategy for advancing the kingdom in society? Or should we be refocusing our efforts and redirecting our energies, so that our church activities are designed to equip people to be Christ's agents for change as they are dispersed into the world twenty-four hours a day, seven days a week?

In an empire model we measure commitment by participation in the activities that we initiate. In a kingdom model we take a wider view. We recognise that we are not the only people of God in our community. We recognise that we are church as much when dispersed as when gathered. We accept a specific responsibility for a geographical area but recognise that the reach of our congregation's influence is far wider. We cooperate with others, unthreatened by the possibility that they may receive fruit rather than us. We do good things because they are right, not simply as a means to an end. We recognise that God is already at work in the world ahead of us.

The paradigm shift from empire to kingdom presents some challenging implications. Effective local churches functioning through the spiritual gifts of the members are not redundant. Committed volunteers will still be required to lead worship, teach children, lead small groups, prepare premises for activities, administer finances, etc. Yet if we think kingdom rather than empire, we will refrain from sustaining a hierarchy that suggests that leadership or service within church structures is more worthy or more spiritual than leadership or service in the community, the marketplace or the home.

The paradigm shift from empire to kingdom challenges the well-meant legalism that regards certain gatherings, such as the midweek prayer meeting, as the benchmark of committed church membership. Involvement in school board, community forum or golf club committee, even while the prayer meeting is taking place, will not be grudgingly tolerated but will become enfranchised as legitimate kingdom activity. In such circumstances those who are available to pray will pray creatively and intelligently for those out on the frontline of mission. Those who are out of town on business will be prayed for as fervently as the overseas missionaries supported by the church.

The paradigm shift from empire to kingdom presents staffing implications for those ministries that have always been run by volunteers. Perhaps a greater range of tasks than before will be carried out by supported staff, releasing other members to the many-faceted opportunities of whole-life ministry. At a very practical level, a cleaning rota may sound like good stewardship, but a paid cleaner may release members for wider involvement. A professional children's worker may provide a preferable alternative to our previous approach to children's ministry. Some such professionals may still be involved in recruiting, equipping and supporting volunteers, but a clear focus of the equipping will recognise 'outside' opportunities for ministry.

This is where a widened application of Ephesians 4:11 comes into play. The arena for the works of service for which apostles, evangelists, prophets, pastors and teachers should equip the people of God will be widened considerably from the current emphasis on internal church activities. The first step in the paradigm shift from the empire of local church to a wider kingdom view will be in the area of vision, awareness and understanding. It will relate to mindset. Casting a vision that includes community engagement and marketplace activity as kingdom business will be essential.

Some years ago I found the Engels scale to be liberating in the area of evangelism.[1] Here was recognition of process, as individuals progressed along a continuum from no marked interest in Christ to full-blown discipleship, with crisis conversion somewhere in the middle. The work of evangelism was understood to be partnership with the Holy Spirit in shifting people along this continuum. Perhaps we need a new scale describing kingdom activity, which may or may not result in personal commitment to Jesus Christ and subsequent full-blown discipleship.

My late wife ran a parent and toddler group in a brand new community in London's Docklands. The wives and partners of young professionals from the City and Docklands were at a loose end once their babies had come along, and socially isolated. They were from many nations, far from home and family-based support systems. It was at the toddler group that they made social contact with people in a similar situation. They would push their prams together around the dock, visiting the local coffee shop. Some holidayed together; some spent Christmas Day together far from their homes in Australia, South Africa, Canada or nearer European nations. Would this be kingdom activity only if they heard an overt Gospel presentation, or is God also at work in these apparently ordinary things? Perhaps if we were to turn our minds to what really constitutes the rule of God in today's world, we might be better placed to answer this question.

Identifying kingdom activities

Changing the definition of what local church is about will therefore be essential. If we don't know what we are aiming for we shall not know if we have hit our target or progressed towards it. Deciding through pastoral interview and mutual accountability which activities can be identified as kingdom activities will become necessary. It is perfectly possible to attend a sports club without any thought of kingdom. In auditing the kingdom activity that takes place, a clear understanding of what we mean by this is necessary. Without it, it is perfectly possible for church members to do their own thing and simply ignore or evade responsibilities they may have to their brothers and sisters. It also demands a church culture of mutual relationship and accountability.

The kingdom / church tension does present a dilemma. The reality is that the argument is one of degree. To what extent should church leadership focus on 'home base' to provide a solid foundation for wider influence? To what extent do we take the radical approach, laying aside some existing and worthwhile ministries, assessing the potential for influence in wider society through the existing activities of the membership? On the basis of such an audit, how do we then commission our members to boldly go into uncharted areas of kingdom potential? And how do we support them once they are there?

Many pastors are seeing the wider picture and casting a vision for a kingdom mindset. But in circles where the local church empire model has prevailed for so long, change is likely to be slow. There is, for example, an inherent inertia in ministerial training and denominational expectation. Furthermore, many Christians are very comfortable with a sacred-secular divide that allows them to compartmentalise church from the rest of life. In this area it is difficult to identify pioneers who can serve as role models for the paradigm shift. Rather we seem to be in a time where fellow travellers must identify one another and find ways of sharing mutual encouragement in the urgent process of turning church inside out to turn the world upside down.

♦ ♦ ♦ ♦

Notes

1. James F. Engel and Wilbert Norton, *What's Gone Wrong with the Harvest?* (Zondervan, 1975).

Questions of leadership

9

What are leaders for?

Paul Weaver

Paul was employed in engineering in the 1960s. He then trained for pastoral ministry and worked as an assistant pastor in Sunderland and as senior leader of a church in Scunthorpe from 1970 to 2002. Since 1984 he has been a lecturer at Mattersey Hall Theological College and a member of the UK Executive of the Assemblies of God. He became an Evangelical Alliance Board member in 1996 and General Superintendent of the Assemblies of God in 1995.

'What are leaders for?' is probably the most important question that could be asked in the context of making disciples who make a difference in today's world. Paul is convinced that the challenge of mobilising God's people is primarily a challenge to leadership. In this chapter he explores seven areas to provoke thought about the role and skills of leaders in disciple-making churches.

For reflection

- How would you answer the question, what are leaders for?
- Which of the seven areas in this chapter do you feel you need to wrestle with most?

What are leaders for?

The question of leadership is one of the most important questions that could be asked in the context of mobilising the body of Christ for service. Good leadership is seen in every successful organisation. The countless books with the word 'leadership' in their titles that can be found in any bookshop reflect the importance of leaders. So why are we here contemplating this question, 'What are leaders for?' and what makes a good leader?[1] My contention is this: when we face the challenge of how we help followers of Christ to become effective in life and mission as his disciples in today's world, that challenge cannot be tackled primarily by focusing on problems or weaknesses within the congregation, but rather through facing issues of leadership within the church. My reflections on this subject come from more than thirty-nine years in leadership in local, regional, national and international contexts. Out of that experience I want to suggest that we need to pay serious attention to the question of 'what leaders are for', since our answer to that question directly shapes the ways in which we might help Christians grow in faith and obedience. In this chapter I shall attempt to provoke answers to that question by stimulating thought in seven areas.

1. Leadership and equipping God's people

In Ephesians 4:11ff we find the universal leadership gifts of the New Testament.[2] This is where we must start if we are to answer the question of what leaders are for. This passage provides fundamental keys to the question of why leaders are given to the church by God, and it illustrates what takes place when all of these gifts work together in harmony for the benefit of the body.

> The gifts he gave were that some would be apostles, some prophets, some evangelists, some pastors and teachers, to equip the saints for the work of ministry, for building up the body of Christ, until all of us come to the unity of the faith and of the knowledge of the Son of God, to maturity, to the measure of the full stature of Christ (Eph. 4:11-13).

Each of the Ephesians 4:11 gifts is given to equip the church for the work of ministry. Therefore any leadership gift that does not train others is abdicating its primary role.

History reveals that leaders have generally performed poorly as equippers of God's people. Where leaders have sought to equip others it has often been with a fairly limited perspective. So, for example, the apostle Paul's injunction in Ephesians 4:11 was to equip the saints through all five leadership gifts. But we have tended to look only to certain leadership gifts, particularly that of the teacher, to equip believers and have often failed to see the potential of other gifts. This alone presents an incredible challenge in today's church. Once we face it, we are presented with all kinds of questions. How might each gift be used to equip others? What does a church look like when it has all five equipping gifts operating in harmony? How is this applied within different church structures, particularly at the small or cell group level? It's good to wrestle with these questions as long as we keep the goal in mind. The role of leadership is to equip the people of God to serve him, and to help others to grow into the fullness of life that reflects the life of our Lord Jesus in today's world. Leaders are disciple-makers.

2. Leadership teams

One of my hobbies is oil painting. To paint effectively, you require different colours; each colour works with the others on the canvas. A leadership team is like a colour palette. If you mix and blend the colours there is a much greater range and depth of colour available for the canvas. In the same way leadership in the Scriptures is always seen in the context of plurality. The diversity of gifts working together in harmony displays the rich mosaic of divine genius. Yet the history of the Christian church reveals a stage littered with lone rangers. Such leaders tend to draw attention to themselves, see themselves as God's answer to the world, and therefore share very few, if any, of the leadership development skills from which others can learn. We must learn how to harness together teams of diversely gifted people.

My current perception of the church is that we still have a lot to learn about equipping the saints through team leadership. Indeed it was only in the middle of the last century that we began to accept team ministry as an essential expression of local church leadership. As I observe the church scene, I see plurality of leadership, but very few teams. And many of the early pioneers of team leadership experienced the fragmentation of their teams because they were slow to learn new lessons.

How does this colour mix of team leadership work? It works primarily through three important ingredients: the recognition of the principle of a 'leader of leaders'; the importance of diversity of gifting; and the importance of a team structure.

a) Leader of leaders

Throughout Scripture we see the principle of a 'leader of leaders'. Such leaders do not have all the answers, but they have the ability to inspire and bring the necessary gifts together to deliver good leadership, in order to execute God's purpose and equip the people.

b) Diversity of gifts
The first thing leaders should do in order to build the right team is to establish what their own gift is. You don't know what you need until you know who and what you are. Duplication of your gift in a team will always result in division. The Ephesians 4:11 text deliberately gives us five different gifts. God's intention for the training of his people is diversity of gifts working together in harmony and with humility.[3]

c) Leadership through teams
Although God gives his leadership gifts to the universal church, they are designed to be used in teams. These teams can be very flexible – they can be local, regional, national or even international. A good team is not just dependent on the mix of gifts, but also on personality and spirituality. Leaders sharpen leaders; leaders can learn from leaders; leaders require other leaders in order to make the most of their own gifts in serving God's people.

3. Leadership and vision

Leaders not only equip but they see tomorrow; they are tomorrow thinkers. This dimension is fundamental to a safe and developing church. Without a vision the people are in disarray, but with a vision people know where they are going. Leadership holds the key to a maturing and purposeful church. Without God-ordained leadership the church is short-sighted. The impact of Jesus was not only what he said and did, but also his insight into things that others were blind to. Jesus knew why he had come into the world and the journey he had to make, as well as the way he would die. His disciples could see a tomorrow, but it was quite different from the one Jesus saw; the people who heard Jesus gladly could often see no further than the need for today's food in their stomachs.

The twenty-first century requires something more than maintenance leadership. Theological colleges come a long way short of honing and delivering tomorrow thinkers. They major in history, theology and counselling at the expense of missional and entrepreneurial leadership that comprehends the creative insights needed to penetrate a lost world. Where are our tomorrow thinkers and where are they in national leadership? The twentieth century has produced national leaders who are products of a past system that has very little cutting edge in the realm of reformation. What are leaders for? Leaders are there to cast a vision for disciple-making that will help the church grow in purpose and in maturity; that will help the church release believers into service and worship in ways that engage holistically and missionally with our culture.

4. Leadership and God's kingdom

New Testament leadership is kingdom-minded. Sadly, this is foreign to our history and to most current leadership thinking and practice. But gone are the days when we concerned ourselves only with one local church or denomination. We may find ourselves mainly operating in one of these realms, but a kingdom mind has an eagle-eye perspective on all who labour for Christ. The kingdom mind knows no competition. The kingdom mind rejoices over the extension of God's kingdom wherever it is and under whatever banner it flourishes. A kingdom mindset acknowledges the importance of interdependence.

1 Corinthians 12 is an excellent exposition of this important issue. We often apply this passage to the local church, but fail to see its application to the church universal. We should challenge all expressions of local church that work independently, because our divisions confuse people outside the church. No wonder Jesus prayed passionately in John 17 for the church to be one. This prayer is made in the context of our oneness in Christ as Christ himself is one with the Father, rooted firmly in the context of mission. Jesus wanted the world to know that God had sent him; he saw the unity of the church as a vital part of that revelation. It is interesting that this prayer was made in the hearing of leaders and not a congregation. Leaders are there to bring this kingdom perspective to the life and mission of their churches.

5. Leadership and mission

All leadership must have a heart for mission, because all Christian leadership should lead people to God. The great challenge of the twenty-first-century church is to place missiology before ecclesiology. This is easily said but quite difficult to do following hundreds of years of tradition, teaching and structure. At times there is more tradition in us than truth. It is very hard to separate tradition from truth.

Jesus always put mission first: the woman at the well was more important than food, companionship with the disciples or even the shortest route to the next destination. The healing of the man with the withered arm was more important than the laws of the Sabbath. The practice of prayer in the temple was more important than its financial maintenance. There are many traditions and practices to break through if we are going to be relevant missional leaders in today's church. There are also some interesting questions we should ask ourselves. How do we reach people? Why do we reach people? What do we say to them when we reach them? What do we teach them when they join the church? How do we develop their God-given skills? How do we cooperate with the Spirit so that we help people experience the Gospel's liberation ever more deeply? How do we help people live as mission-hearted disciples of Christ? Leadership is there to wrestle with these questions and to engage the church in working answers to them into the life of the church community.

6. Leadership and effective communication

Good leadership is about strategy and process: where we want to go and how we are going to get there. Jesus' commission to us is clear – we are to make disciples. The good news we have to share is profound. But our delivery of this message is too often ineffective. Leadership is crucial to the delivery of the message. But what do I mean by this? I'm not just referring to obvious communication channels such as preaching, although that is often sadly lacking in terms of contemporary communication. Nor am I primarily focusing on what we communicate through our gatherings in church, through the building itself, or the language we use or the way we dress and so on, though they do indeed impact people in a significant way. Rather I'm referring to the many ways in which the Christian message is conveyed to non-believers both individually and at a societal level through the lives that Christians lead; whether those lives are authentic or not; whether they are holistic and reflect the myriad dimensions of being human; whether they have moral integrity; whether they reflect a daily freshness in the Spirit. Leadership is there to help God's people become witnesses, effective communicators of a whole-life Gospel message to the people and the culture that they can influence. Leaders have an enormously significant role in helping people to live integrated and authentic lives that increasingly reflect the good news of God's comprehensive salvation. And they have a role to play in helping people connect this message to a contemporary context.

7. Leadership and the next generation

Historically, local churches have gone up and down numerically with every change of leader. Churches have moved from one vision to another and lost ground through this process, in terms of both people and time. The challenge today is to move to transitional leadership, moving from generation to generation with consistent values endorsed by successive local leaders. This has implications for the methods used to appoint leaders to churches and brings the responsibility of people development back to the local church. It does not negate the importance of theological colleges, but it does challenge those colleges to think differently about how and why they exist.

Transitional leadership highlights the importance of team leadership in the local church. We have already established that team is more than plurality; it is the composite of different kinds of people and gifts working together for a purpose bigger than any one individual. It is through the team that leadership development is progressed. Although there is a 'leader of leaders' within the team, that leader is more interested in the success of their successors than in their own personal success. A primary leadership task is to produce the next generation of leaders who will espouse the same values, if not the same methods, of mission to the world.

Conclusion

What are leaders for? They are given by God to lead and mature the church for action. The Great Commission directs that action. Leadership is therefore undertaken in the light of the mission needs of our nation. What does our nation need? It needs Christians who are prepared to live out a radical discipleship that engages with the questions of our culture; a discipleship that reflects what it means to be truly human; a discipleship that counts the cost yet is prepared to pay it for the sake of the kingdom. Leaders are there to equip the people of God for their calling to be followers of Jesus in today's world, to be mission-hearted disciples of Christ. Leaders are there to cast such a vision, to help the church release believers into service and worship in ways that engage holistically and missionally with our culture. Leaders are there to help people to learn to live integrated and authentic lives that increasingly reflect the good news of God's comprehensive salvation. Leaders are there to work as a team with others, harnessing a diversity of gifting so that they can be faithful to their calling to be equippers of the saints from generation to generation.

♦ ♦ ♦ ♦

Notes

1 See also chapter 10: Leadership matters.
2 See also chapter 3: Ephesians 4 ministries and spiritual formation.
3 See Greg Haslam on humility in chapter 3.

10

Leadership matters: developing leaders for the disciple-making church

James Lawrence

James is CPAS Director for the Arrow Leadership Programme and its founder in the UK and Ireland. Ordained, and an evangelist, trainer and author, he works with churches and leaders to develop missional leadership. Most recently he has piloted and now launched Growing Leaders, *a practical training resource adapted from the Arrow Leadership Programme, to help churches grow leaders.*

If we're to invest in growing healthy disciple-making communities we'll need to invest in growing healthy disciple-making leaders. Leadership matters. In this chapter James explores the issues in developing effective leadership and highlights some directions for regenerating leadership training today.

For reflection

- How does the way we develop leaders shape the way we make disciples for today's world?
- In the light of this chapter, how would you evaluate the leadership training in your church?

Leadership matters: developing leaders for the disciple-making church

I was 13. I'd just come to faith in Christ outside a church context. I was idealistic, energetic, arrogant, and hungry to grow. I wanted to learn how to be a disciple of Jesus Christ. I spent three years looking for help. I tried the Christian Union at school, the local church (lowering the average age by forty years when I walked through the door), reading the Bible (must have something to do with Christianity), and prayer. You wouldn't believe how difficult it was to find someone who would talk to me about Jesus in a way I could understand. Yet here I am nearly thirty years later, ordained and trying to do everything I can to help others discover the wonderful realities of a life lived in relationship with God as Trinity.

What eventually helped me through? Christians who recognised the value of the disciple-making process and committed themselves to making the local church a disciple-making community.

Over the years since then, and through my work around the country, I've become convinced that one of the key factors in helping churches to make disciples is effective leadership. Some recent research conducted by the Natural Church Development Network identified 'empowering leadership' as one of the eight factors commonly found in growing, healthy churches.[1] Yet it also identified this as the factor that scored lowest in a survey of British churches. The thesis of this chapter is that if we are to grow healthy, disciple-making communities we'll need to invest in growing healthy, disciple-making leaders. To 'let my people grow' we will need to grow people as leaders. Why? Four reasons:

1. Leaders influence people, for good or bad. The vision and values of the leader(ship) of a local church will impact the direction and culture of the church. If the leader is not committed to developing a disciple-making church it is unlikely the church will move far in this direction.
2. In a time of significant cultural change the leader's job is more complex. Many church leaders are struggling with the job and are looking for help to lead well.
3. People rarely go beyond their leader. It is a sobering truth, but one which leaders come to recognise. If the leader stops growing, so will the people.
4. There is a shortage of people willing to step forward to lead. Most local churches experience this shortage when trying to recruit leaders. Some denominations are also experiencing this at a national level. For example, the Church of England struggles to recruit younger people to the ordained ministry. We need to grow the leaders we have, *and* to grow more leaders.

So what are the issues we face if we are to develop leaders for the disciple-making church and what can we do about them?

Leading learners

Discipleship is caught as much as it is taught. This is not to undermine the importance of teaching, but rather to expand a sometimes too narrow view of teaching as solely a didactic process. People learn in a variety of ways, and one of the most significant influences on people's lives is the model they see before them. The practical outworking of this is seen in congregations that over time come to reflect their minister. Therefore if we desire to grow disciple-making churches, the leaders need to continue as disciples themselves. Obvious? Maybe. Yet those of us in church leadership know how easy it is to become stuck, no longer growing in our own personal discipleship because the demands and difficulties of the job have all but squeezed out time for basic discipleship and the hope of change.

We see this at CPAS in the leadership development programme we run (Arrow).[2] We work with church leaders between the ages of 25 and 45. They are gifted and committed people. Yet many of them struggle with basic discipleship issues. Little time for prayer or Bible study; no regular pattern of quiet days / space; infrequent use of spiritual disciplines; no time or energy for personal growth and development; unresolved internal issues; growing frustration with the lack of personal change; many falling at the hurdles of mid-ministry transition.[3]

We need growing leaders to lead growing churches. We need leaders who are learners, committed to lifelong growth and development. We need strategies and structures that promote growth in personal discipleship as an essential part of what it means to be a Christian leader. Some denominations are moving towards this, with an increasing number of initiatives to promote this approach. My hunch is that we need both to develop a mindset that encourages such personal development as part of the life of a minister and to back it up with sufficient resources to make it possible. Ad hoc day conferences are simply not enough.

Where will this start? From the top and the bottom. From the top, because senior leaders who model this will influence those under their jurisdiction. From the bottom, because if we can grow leaders with this attitude, and help them to keep it, they will enter a lifelong process as a leading learner. Three things are at the heart of this approach: growing self-awareness, a process that enables change to take place, and a leadership model rooted in discipleship.

Growing self-awareness

I'm not here advocating an unhealthy, introspective navel-gazing. Self-obsession quickly leads to self-absorption. Rather, a healthy biblical understanding of what Paul was alluding to when he said, 'Watch your life and doctrine closely' (1 Tim. 4:16, NIV). There is a right self-awareness that is found through openness to the Holy Spirit, reflection on the Scriptures and feedback from those around us. Increased self-awareness can fuel ongoing growth and development through a willingness to face up to some of the realities about ourselves and hear the voice of Jesus inviting us on to become more like him. This is an essential part of discipleship.

On its own, though, this will probably not be enough. The danger is that most of us are either naively optimistic about ourselves or unnecessarily pessimistic. Some of us veer towards being too soft on ourselves, others too hard. So this growing self-awareness is greatly aided by a context that enables change to take place.

A place to change

It is frightening how many church leaders work in relative isolation. Speaking on the phone yesterday to a church leader, I heard her recount how in fourteen years of ordained ministry she had had only two reviews and one enquiry about her well-being. For some this isolation is self-imposed, for others it's part of the system. I'm convinced that the biblical model of leadership in community is the first issue we need to address.[4] But beyond that, it would help to provide places for people to change, contexts in which honesty, vulnerability, self-reflection, learning and growth take place. A number of leadership development programmes are experimenting with this to great effect. My hope is that initiatives such as these will become part of the normal provision for church leaders.

A model to work with

As we seek to grow disciple-making churches, we need leaders whose own understanding of leadership reflects the breadth of the biblical picture. That not only means leaders of different ages, types, backgrounds, cultures and genders, but also leaders who grapple with the realities of an integrated discipleship model.

Christian leadership flows out of Christian discipleship. All those who are part of Christ's body are called to the lifelong transformative process of following Jesus. Part of that life is ministry (serving), a particular expression of discipleship. Each person takes up the emblem of the follower of Jesus, the towel, and serves those around them by using their gifts to bless others. Within this wider orbit of ministry are a variety of specific callings and gifts, one of which is leadership. So we cannot divorce leadership from its roots in discipleship and the trunk of ministry.

Therefore it helps if the model for developing leaders reflects this, and provides a pattern for discipleship development.

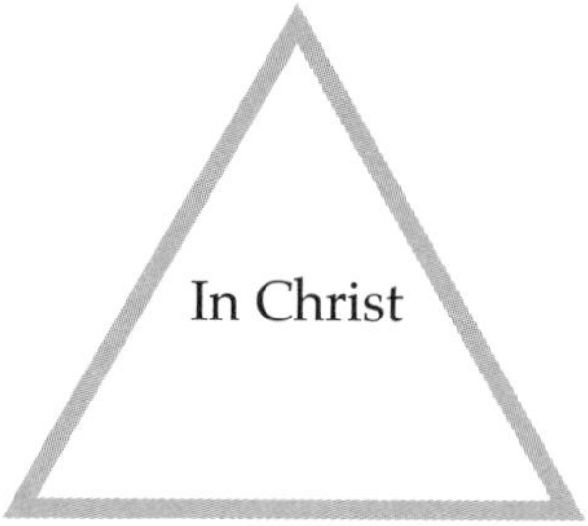

At its heart is recognition of our covenant relationship with God through Christ by the Holy Spirit. If we are not 'in Christ' or unsure of who we are in him (Eph. 1:3-14), the heart is not well, and that influences everything else. Sadly, some in leadership struggle to accept for themselves the very truths they preach to others – grace, forgiveness and security in Christ. That's why some leaders' lifestyles model inappropriate ways of living the Christian life, in particular drivenness and a dependence on doing rather than being for security and self-worth. This is the core of understanding the Christian faith, and therefore at the heart of discipleship and Christian leadership. It is not about us, who we are; it is about God and who we are 'in Christ'.

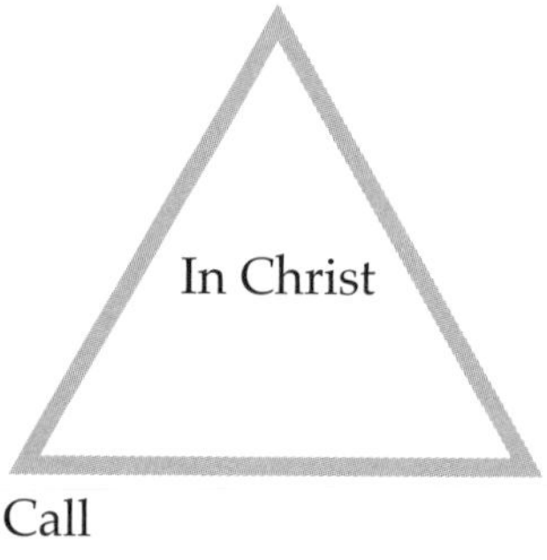

With the heart working well, the foundation for a Christian understanding of leadership development comprises call and character. Call is a sense of God's direction for our lives that affects not only the big decisions concerning what to do with our life, but also the smaller details of how we spend our time this week, this day, this hour. So many struggle to balance their lives between competing demands on their time and attention. The clearer we are about God's call, and the more we start to experience how that call brings focus to our lives, the more we are able to see that a balanced life is not even a biblical concept and to give ourselves to the things that God wants as our priority.

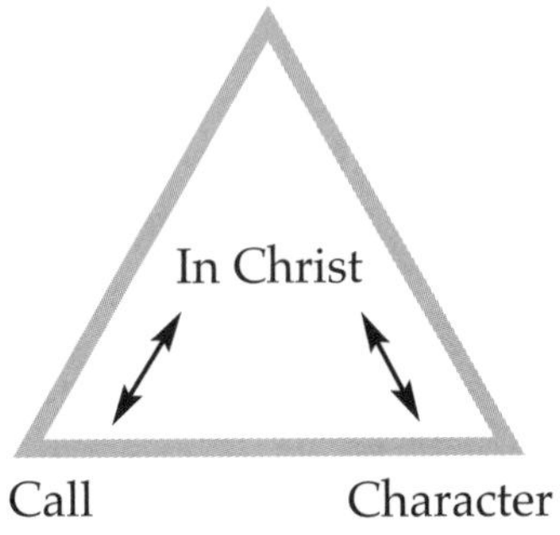

Character is a life that reflects Christlikeness. It focuses on godliness. So many of the things that scupper people in leadership are rooted in character issues. The major emphasis of the pastoral epistles is on these character traits. Within this area I find it helpful to make a distinction between character and personality, because it influences our expectations about change. Whilst I recognise that there is a large 'grey area' between personality and character, personality is the basic building block of who we are, focused around preferences. Each human being has preferences because of the way they are wired up, which is a combination of nature and nurture. Such preferences are generally in place by adulthood. Personality is value-neutral. One type of personality isn't 'better' than another, it's just different. If we view personality in this way, we recognise that our personality can be polished like a pearl, but not changed very much. Therefore growing self-awareness (maturity) is vital, because it helps us better understand our preferences and how they impact others.

Character is the aggregate of the distinctive qualities characteristic of an individual. Character contains a value judgement, which is why we speak of a person of good or bad character. As Christians we believe God wants to grow us in Christlike character, in qualities such as godliness, integrity, faithfulness, humility, truthfulness, servant-heartedness. These are not preferences or optional extras, but an essential part of following Christ. One of the dangers is that the demands of our ministry can exceed our maturity of character. We need to be humble about our strengths and prayerfully intentional about our weaknesses, allowing Christ to transform us. Our model of developing leaders must focus on character issues as much as the skills required for leadership, otherwise once again we may grow leaders who model a false picture of discipleship and ministry. As the theologian Peter Kuzmic put it, 'Charisma without character leads to catastrophe.'

There is an additional element to the foundation – confidence. There is an appropriate confidence to leadership, located in who we are in Christ, founded on a clear sense of God's call, fuelled by a healthy understanding of ourselves, and strengthened as we develop skills and a track record. In work done to develop women in leadership this aspect has proved particularly important.[5]

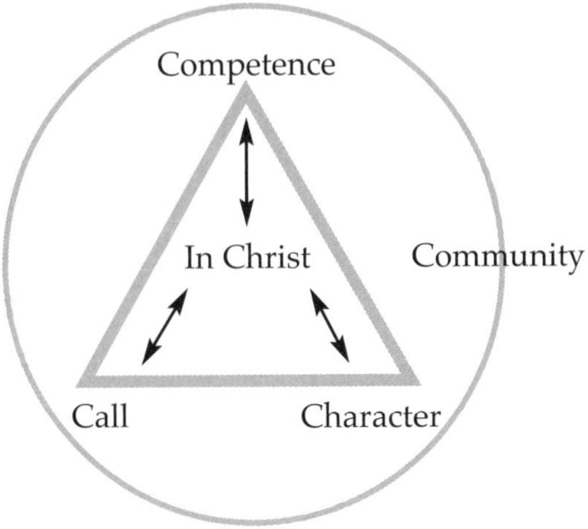

A strong foundation supports the development of appropriate skills (competence) in leadership. We don't just make all people of good character leaders. There are certain traits to effective leadership, a combination of talents, skills and knowledge, some of which can be taught. Ideally the best context for the growth of leadership is one of Christian community. When we enable leaders to grow in this context we model to them the primacy of community in the disciple-making process.

This model helps us to recognise that the roots of leadership development are indeed in discipleship issues. How we develop leaders will influence how we develop disciples and vice versa. They are inextricably linked. We cannot talk about whole-life disciple-making without reflecting on our leadership patterns. We cannot develop leaders without building into the foundations essential discipleship processes. Healthy leadership development reflects this intricate relationship.

There are three challenges I'd like to identify in order to stimulate discussion and exploration about how we can best resource church leaders in the way we train them.

Issue 1. The priority of embodiment and the problem of how this can be done if the leader is 'full-time' in this role

We may want to shift the focus of church life to whole-life discipleship, but if the minister's life is completely wrapped up with the local church (it is their place of work, often the primary community they belong to), how can they embody this vision? Some experiment with other models. A friend of mine went from being a paid church minister to being a paid part-time ophthalmologist and part-time unpaid minister. However, the demands of the two worlds became too much and he has returned to being a paid full-time church minister.

I wonder if what is at fault here is the continuing predominance of the model of a solo person as church leader, which places untold demands on any individual, when the New Testament pattern is a community model of leadership. Despite this, I think many church leaders will be full-time. So how are they to embody whole-life discipleship?

- In their relating: church leaders need to go to where the people are. Simply visiting people in their place of work is a start. It takes time and effort, but is such a rewarding experience as you involve yourself in some small way in the world where people spend large amounts of their time.
- In their learning: if we are to engage with the issues that people are grappling with in the whole of life,

it will help if we read widely, observe carefully and listen thoughtfully.

- In their teaching and training: language and illustrations are telling. We will more readily connect with people if we use stories from their worlds, make applications that relate to Monday to Saturday lives, and deal with the issues they face.
- In their leading: church leaders who focus on church may miss the breadth of the kingdom issues we are called to grapple with. It is too easy for a local congregation to be centripetal rather than centrifugal, sucking life into the centre rather than distributing life liberally. The church is the gathered / sent community. Church leadership is about resourcing people to be Christians on Monday to Sunday, to make a difference in the world.

Issue 2. Teaching and training

If church leaders are called to 'equip the saints for the work of ministry' (Eph. 4:12), what is the best way of doing this? Elsewhere in this book others reflect on this issue from the disciple-making aspect. I will restrict my comment to the leadership element. One issue may be that most of us were 'equipped to lead' in fairly limited ways, setting up a model that might not best prepare us to equip others. I know that theological colleges and courses are making significant changes in this area, and I certainly don't want to minimise the importance of theological education. It is vital that we have leaders who can think, reflect and act theologically. But what I want to encourage is conversation about the methods we use to do this, so that the wide range of people needed within church leadership can be encouraged to come forward and those in church leadership can 'catch' how to equip others. Disciple-making is a proactive, intentional process involving a variety of approaches. Jesus models it for us. What if ministerial training reflected his model a little more closely?

Issue 3. The focus of disciple-making

Too often church leaders tend to 'default to adult', to think primarily about the discipling needs of adults within their congregations. Indeed in practice this can sometimes become a focus on a certain age range, normally around the age of the church leader! Yet the church is a body made up of children, young people and adults of all ages. Disciple-making must include all these people. Children and young people who aren't simply entertained at church but enabled to be radical followers of Jesus from their earliest days. Senior citizens who aren't simply 'put up with' but enabled to be radical followers of Jesus till their dying day. For at every stage and every age there is an appropriate relationship with Jesus. I would urge us to continue reflecting on how we do this, particularly with children and young people. These are the formative years, and sadly they are often lost to genuine spiritual development. We give young people a very inadequate view of discipleship, which keeps them in church but never helps them to be the church at school, at college, at home or in the workplace. These are also the formative years for leadership development.

Let our leaders grow

Contemporary leadership development is in an exciting place. We have the opportunity to shape things for the future. The models and methods we use will influence the disciple-making potential of the church. For the sake of those who don't know Christ, let's grow more leaders who continue to grow as disciples, growing disciple-making churches. Leadership matters.

♦ ♦ ♦ ♦

Further reading and resources

Jinkins, Michael, *Transformational Ministry: Church Leadership and the Way of the Cross* (St Andrew Press, 2003)

Mallison, John, *Mentoring to Develop Disciples and Leaders* (SU, 1998)

Nouwen, Henri, *In the Name of Jesus* (DLT, 1989)

Wright, Walter, *Relational Leadership: a Biblical Model for Leadership Service* (Paternoster, 2000)

To find out more about the CPAS leadership development resource *Growing Leaders* visit www.cpas.org.uk/growing or telephone CPAS on 01926 458458.

Notes

1 NDC News-sheet 18.

2 www.cpas.org.uk/arrow

3 For further details see James Lawrence, *Growing Leaders* (BRF, 2004).

4 See Gilbert Bilezikian, *Community 101: Reclaiming the Church as a Community of Oneness* (Zondervan, 1997); Gordon Fee, *Listening to the Spirit in the Text* (Eerdmans, 2000).

5 See www.nextlevelleadership.ca

Responding to human diversity

11

The human disciple

Brian Draper

Previously editor of the Christian current affairs magazine Third Way, *Brian is now Lecturer in Contemporary Culture at LICC. His postgraduate research in postmodernity and ecclesiology underpins his quest to find how Christians can engage biblically with culture in a rapidly changing world. Brian is also a freelance writer and a pioneer in the alternative worship movement.*

Human discipleship is not simply an academic exercise or an ecclesiological enterprise. It's only incarnated, truly fleshed out, through our complex relationships with each other, the planet, ourselves and our God. In this chapter Brian explores a vision for communities that long to become more fully human in Christ and to help others start living life – to the full.

For reflection

- How curious are you about this journey of following Jesus?
- How would you describe what it means to be fully human in Christ?

The human disciple

One of the effects of the splintering of the church into tribes and micro-cultures is that people of different types and shades of belief seem less inclined to learn from each other. (When I grew up, I thought that most people in most of the other churches in our small town weren't even Christian.) We've also, in particular, separated the generations, which has slowed the process of learning from each other. Of course, the rending in twain of the old, the not-quite-so old and the young first began out in the world at large. We created the popular cult of youth and, meanwhile, dispatched the elderly to scrabble away their days together in the local home. Grannies were great for dispensing sweets, but not wisdom. The nuclear family, just like society, became ever more atomised, before we split . . .

Our parents, the first generation to wrestle in earnest with the task of raising culture-surfing teenagers, couldn't quite understand the clothes and sounds and words and protests of the baby busters. So they handed remote control to the TV presenters, pop stars, icons and advertisers, who did understand because they were part of the same generation. The kids, meanwhile, deciphered from the TV presenters, pop stars, icons and advertisers that it wasn't cool to grow old or become like your parents. Anyway, what can you learn from ageing hippies who are stuck in a faraway world of Moon landings and Morris Minors – apart from how not to do it?

The wisdom of age and experience ceased to flow from old to young. The wide-eyed wonder of childhood perception, together with a slightly less reverential attitude to received wisdom, ceased to flow from young to old. And the church bought into this, wholesale. Or is that retail? Of course, there were good reasons, the main one being that you couldn't expect young people to have to pitch up at many of the types of church that were on offer. But in the process, we lost a little of the humanity that's generated in the creaturely act of relating together.

The divine flow of the Spirit of God was dammed; it struggled to find a channel through which to pour between those of different age, creed and colour (though you can never stop the work of the Spirit entirely). We appreciated less the *difference* of the other, and began to settle into a cultural and spiritual routine – of uniformity and tribalism within Christian subcultures – even within the most contemporary forms of church. Cultural uniformity, if we're not careful, can further dehumanise us. We begin to lose our identity as individuals relating within a diverse community of people, a group that's held in place by a proactive love for each other's differences, not just their similarities.

To become a Christian, how must I become more like you, as well as more like Christ?

It's a crucial discipleship question, as we've an amazing call: to model a new way of being and becoming more fully human to a watching world, a world that's asking the age-old question 'Who am I?' within new, challenging contexts today. But we tend to muddle it, sometimes, by insisting that people look, speak and act like us culturally before they can belong. And that's not the point of discipleship. Neither is human discipleship simply an academic exercise or an ecclesiological enterprise. It's not just a word, an idea, or a chapter in a book. Like most theoretical concepts it's only truly fleshed out – incarnated, if we want to be technical – through our complex network of relationships with each other, the planet, ourselves and our God. It's about passing on and receiving wisdom for the united journey of faith and life. It's about being willing to learn from each other – a very different practice from being ready to teach people a thing or two.

We need to *learn* to *listen*. We need to *listen* to *learn*. Not just to the voice of the one expert at the front, the dispenser of facts and God-breathed propositions, but to the different voices within the whole community of believers, and sometimes to those outside. Are we genuinely curious about the people we might want to disciple?

One example of learning together across the generations that I've recently experienced is 'Godly Play'. Godly Play is a more open-ended form of storytelling for children, in which you tell them a Bible story but don't immediately shut down the possibilities of the story by explaining the moral of the tale. Instead, once you've told the story, with a few props to help, you have a time of wondering together about the characters, the outcome, the possibilities of the story. You then break for a time of creative response, in which the children paint, draw, model clay, and do all sorts of other creative things. Godly Play is an excellent example of an act of gathered worship that can be truly inter-generational if we let it. If the adults will join in. It works so long as the older people are willing to put on hold their assumptions about the story, and come to it afresh through the eyes of a child.

Jesus said that we must become like little children in order to enter the kingdom of God. How can we learn from children? And how can we facilitate the mutual process of learning together as a family, rather than coming to learn knowledge and facts from someone who talks at you and sends you away? Discipleship is about exchanging our wisdom within the family of God. If we develop homogeneous subcultures that merely reflect those of the world, our communities will become more like caricatures of ourselves and less like the multi-faceted diamond of a God we claim to worship. It's a challenge to us, but a wonderful opportunity to actively nurture inclusivity within our communities, and to celebrate each other's differences. Culture can learn from culture; generation can challenge and encourage generation; denomination can love denomination; and we can begin to grow up. Our discipleship does not need to be stunted. We can flourish, not diminish, as *people*.

A commercial break

One thing we need to beware is an all-consuming consumerist mentality. We try to see the world through Christian eyes, but it's not easy when we all breathe the air of late capitalism. So it's hard not to measure spiritual success in terms of numbers and appearance, for example, or to judge services by the way they make us feel. But we must remember to cherish quality, not just quantity, especially when it comes to relationships.

I remember once seeing a Christian t-shirt that said 'Jesus saves in an instant – everyone's a winner!' It mimicked the National Lottery adverts of the time, and was quite a clever play on words. But it also betrayed the tendency of Christians to look for the quick fix, the instant hit, and to offer it as a means of mission. The result is that we are in danger of remaining resolutely adolescent about life and faith when we should be providing a counter-cultural model of how to walk the longer, slower path towards maturity and spiritual depth. In our discipleship there is clearly a tension to work out between maturing in Christ and approaching him like a child.

My fear, now, is that even our older generations of people are stuck in a kind of consumerist moment, afraid or unequipped to move beyond the first flush of their spirituality – one that celebrates Jesus variously as a romantic lover, a superhero and a genie we can summon at the flick of our fingers to rid us of our troubles.

Towards integrity

It's not that we don't experience the trials of life; God knows, we're all up against it. Whether we face tragedy head-on or are simply negotiating our way through another work-stuffed week, we all, to one degree or another, struggle along with the flipside of life. The problem is we can also struggle, quite fairly, to apply our faith to the trials, because our faith doesn't always match up to our life's experience. Instead of moving together beyond the initial, more brittle stages of faith into a deeper, slightly more permeable spirituality – which takes us further into the riches of Christ's teaching, the open-endedness of his parables, the tension of his metaphors – we can, if we're not careful, remain rigidly conformed to the faith of our first impressions.

And so, when things go wrong, we can put our life and belief into two separate compartments as a coping mechanism. And rarely the twain shall meet again. The human disciple is split in two, into the Christian and the everyday Jo or Brian. We lose, in essence, our integrity as human beings. Thankfully, in Jesus we have the model of the one human who walked with complete integrity. We can't hope to integrate every part of our life into one seamless flow of spiritual excellence this side of eternity, but we can move positively towards that goal, as we seek to be transformed into the likeness of Christ.

Moving on

If we begin to see faith more as a journey (and less as a set of boxes to tick), and if we see the people in our communities as travellers together on that journey, then the process of developing and nurturing our faith can become more dynamic, purposeful, creative, adventurous and ongoing. We embrace the challenge of taking one another beyond a certain faith stage to a place where we can cope more fully with the tensions and hard questions that arise from walking the narrow path of Christ. James Fowler talks of six 'stages of faith'. 'We do find many persons, in churches and out, who are best described by faith that essentially took form when they were adolescents.'[1] As we grow older, we hope also to grow wiser: in life *and* in faith. There's a difference between being experienced Christians, who've read all the books, got all the worship tapes and been to all the meetings, and being experienced human beings who are equipped to live life differently, positively, creatively, purposefully as followers of Christ.

If we are to grow, both as communities and individuals, we need to help people to understand that by questioning and moving on from the first days of their belief, they are not betraying their faith, their roots or even their God. They are going deeper into the mystery of life and faith as a follower of Christ. I would like to be able to say, along with the author Mike Riddell, that 'the Way of Christ, out of which I live, is not a closed perspective but an open one. It suggests a continuous surging creative drive at work in the world, which is relentlessly transforming life.'[2]

One thing I must confess at this point: I'm not keen on the word 'discipleship'. It's one of those words that either seems to have negative connotations (for discipleship read 'heavy shepherding') or else it's become jargon for a programmatic form of church that says little to me about my life. It's important to cut through perceptions and jargon to reclaim something beautiful and biblical. It's also important to guard against putting things in neat boxes. Take the idea, for example, that mission ends at conversion, when discipleship begins. If we see our lives and our faith as one continuous journey, we can see more clearly that mission and discipleship remain positively intertwined. Discipleship, surely, is the act or the art of following Christ. When we make a decision for Christ, we haven't completely arrived. Of course, we are justified by faith, and we can celebrate reaching a high point on our journey. But as soon as we arrive at that point, Jesus' response is simple: Follow me. Our journey along the Way, along the narrow path, begins in earnest.

Following Christ is not about becoming like the stereotypical Christian – it's about starting to explore and inhabit the words of Jesus, who said that he had come so that we might have life, and life to the full. The moment we cease being curious, the moment we stop journeying along the Way, we start diminishing, not growing. Discipleship is not about being told what to do, but about being shown how to live. It's not about developing a neat programme which formulates all the right answers, but about recognising that every step along the way of life is crucial, that our lives matter to God as a whole, not just on the whole.

It's about learning to live together according to the topsy-turvy values of the kingdom – in which the first will be last, and the last first. To demonstrate to each other, in dialogue, conversation and action as we travel together, how Jesus intended us to live. What did he mean, for example, when he said that 'whoever holds on to his life will lose it, but whoever loses it for my sake will find it'? I don't want you just to tell me – I want you to show me. In fact, I want to try and work it out together, within my community, in an atmosphere of mutual accountability, not power.

Searching for a reason

I don't know about you, but for me it starts with first things first: I want to know why I should even get out of bed in the morning. Have you got a raison d'être? What is it, in a sentence? What do you want written as your epitaph – a succinct phrase or sentence that sums you up, that tells a passer-by in a hundred years' time how you lived? I love the Christian Aid strap-line 'We believe in life before death.' I can't wait to get to heaven; but I *can't* wait to get to heaven to start living.

I don't want to be a Christian who is schooled in the intricacies of church life but who can't show others how to transform themselves and the world around them. I want to be more like Bono, who sang, 'I'm not afraid to die; I'm not afraid to live.' I want to be more like Bono, because I see in him something of Christ's guts, passion, eloquence and actions. Ultimately, I want to become more like Christ, but I sense that he points towards the Way.

I dream of a day when the artists, the creative types, the misfits and the life-livers can find a home within the community of believers, because it has transformed, gloriously, into a melting pot of culture. I dream of the day we talk the talk and then proceed to speak God's richness, wholeness and creativity into being with our lives. Because I, for one, still feel the need to grow deeper, to learn the art of living according to the way of Christ from those who have walked the path before me with greater integrity.

How, then, shall we live?

I dream of being part of a band of believers who are willing to follow Jesus out of the church and into the workplace, into our home life, into our art, our music, our writing, our fashion, our passion, our consumer choices, our lives *as a whole*.

I dream of being part of a band of believers who encourage each other to get up in the morning and face the sacredness of the day – in all its mundane, remarkable beauty. Who see the word of life pulsing through our veins, and coursing through creation.

Elizabeth Wurtzel wrote in her best-selling book *Prozac Nation*, 'You wake up one morning afraid you're going to live.'[3] Our high-street bookshops are heaving with life-coaching manuals. I fully believe that people want to start learning to live again. They're tired of disconnected lives, of sensing that they are dislocated from the planet, each other, themselves and God. But they don't always know where to look to find life as intended by the Creator – life that is lived to the full. We can show to a watching world that following Christ makes a difference, not just to us, but to others, to the planet, to God. So long, of course, as it does. And we'll only do that more effectively when we start showing each other first, creating radical communities that are willing to change as they listen to and learn from each other.

As we follow Jesus, the divine face of authentic humanity, not only do we set about doing the Father's business, but also we begin the journey of discovering what it means to be transformed into the likeness of the God-made-fully-human. If we downplay the humanity of Christ, we diminish our own humanity. Conversely, each time we follow in his footsteps, each time we hold to his teaching and begin to walk in the truth, each time we sense the freedom that comes with being his disciple, we continue along the path of personal and social transformation that we believe will be made complete, one glorious day.

In his wonderful book *Being Human, Being Church* Robert Warren writes

> The Good News, as it relates to our culture, is that being fully human has been demonstrated for us in the person of Jesus Christ, made accessible to us through baptismal incorporation into his death, resurrection, ascension and the gift of the Holy Spirit, and – how wonderful it would be if we could add! – is now being incarnately demonstrated at your nearest local church. The prophetic word for our culture is about God's way of being human.[4]

Discipleship? It's profoundly simple, but simply profound. It's about becoming more fully human in Christ, in all the radical, upside-down ways that entails, and helping others to start living life – to the full.

♦ ♦ ♦ ♦

Further reading

Draper, Brian, *Searching 4 Faith* (Lion, 2006)
Riddell, Mike, *The Sacred Journey* (Lion, 2001)
Warren, Robert, *Being Human, Being Church* (Marshall Pickering, 1995)
Wurtzel, Elizabeth, *Prozac Nation* (Quartet, 1996)

Notes

1. James W. Fowler, *Stages of Faith: The Psychology of Human Development and the Quest for Meaning* (Harper and Row, 1971).
2. Mike Riddell, *The Sacred Journey* (Lion, 2001).
3. Elizabeth Wurtzel, *Prozac Nation* (Quartet, 1996).
4. Robert Warren, *Being Human, Being Church* (Marshall Pickering, 1996).

12

As a young person, what would Jesus do?

Jason Gardner

Jason Gardner is youth researcher at the London Institute for Contemporary Christianity. He is currently seeking to tie in trends in secular youth culture with how the church approaches the issue of reaching out to today's generation. Prior to joining LICC Jason completed degrees in English and Theology and has worked alongside young people in and outside the church. He is also involved with Romance Academy, *a sex and relationship education programme for teens, which inspired the BBC2 programme* No sex please, we're teenagers.

It's vital that we embrace a vision of disciple-making that encompasses every area of life – and young people need to be discipled too. In this chapter Jason explores the importance of intergenerational, holistic disciple-making, presenting an alternative perspective on youth work and highlighting the critical importance of adult role modelling.

For reflection

- What do adults model about discipleship in your church community?
- Would any of the ten ideas at the end of the chapter be helpful in your context?

As a young person, what would Jesus do?

> After three days they found him in the temple courts, sitting among the teachers, listening to them and asking them questions. And all who heard him were amazed at his understanding and his answers. When his parents saw him they were astonished; and his mother said to him, 'Child, why have you treated us like this? Look, your father and I have been searching for you in great anxiety.'
>
> He said to them, 'Why were you searching for me? Did you not know that I must be in my Father's house?' But they did not understand what he said to them.
>
> Then he went down with them and came to Nazareth, and was obedient to them. His mother treasured all these things in her heart. And Jesus increased in wisdom and in years, and in divine and human favour (Lk. 2:46-52).

How do we help young people learn to live well for Christ? How can our church communities envision, equip and support young people to grow in faith and in wisdom for life in today's world? When we turn to both the Old and New Testaments, the insights we gain there on 'discipling' young people present a major challenge to our contemporary approaches to this task. In Old Testament passages such as Deuteronomy 6 we see that both the family and the wider community assume responsibility for the nurture and training of the next generation. In the New Testament, Luke's description of the young Jesus with the teachers at the temple may be a unique record of a 'wisdom exchange' between generations. But it is unlikely to have been a unique experience for Jesus. The rhythm of community life around the synagogue, regular annual visits to the temple and the rigours of memorising the Torah would all have contributed to a process of maturing in faith and life. In addition to his own parents, Jesus would have had many other 'significant' adults who embraced their responsibility in shaping him and his contemporaries.

Luke's account of this temple incident points to another significant challenge for the discipleship of young people today. Jesus at 12 is only one birthday away from becoming an adult. In Jesus' day, as is the case with most pre-industrialised societies, there was a clear distinction between child and adult. There was no 'limbo' period in between – the limbo period we call adolescence or 'troubled teens'. This meant the elders at the temple knew exactly what their role was in relation to a 12-year-old Jewish male about to become an adult. Today the boundaries between childhood and adulthood are blurred. As a result we are no longer so clear about the role we should play when confronted with an 8-year-old girl who dresses like a 16-year-old, who in turn dresses exactly the way she is told to by *Cosmopolitan* magazine or her friends. It's even more confusing when we're outside the immediate family and our authority over younger members of our community is not clearly defined.

What is more, the way we view our youth – as children, adolescents or young adults – will entirely shape how we disciple young people. David Wilson of Agape, the campus evangelism organisation, once commented, 'Teenagers are being taught nuclear physics at school and gentle Jesus meek and mild on a Sunday. No wonder so many drift away from Christianity when they get to university.' In the main, we've not equipped our young people to handle the intellectual challenges they will meet as young adults, let alone resourced them spiritually and emotionally with the disciplines, courage and resilience to be able to grow through the experiences of early adulthood.

Schools allegedly prepare young people for the adult world of work. A discipleship model that embraces whole-life Christianity would seek to prepare our young people for the challenges they might face as an adult. We believe that God is interested in all of life – work, rest, relationships, eating, drinking, playing – so how do we give our young people a faith framework with which they can tackle life's issues? And when it comes to making young people whole-life disciples of Christ, what are the challenges we have to overcome today?

A changing world

A quick examination of the backdrop to nurturing faith amongst the young in the UK today might have us wrestling with the following problems:

- There is no longer an assumption that adults are authorities when it comes to any subject, be it fashion or faith.
- Society, the church included, is obsessed with addressing niche age groups in order to appeal to the specific needs and wants of each group's demographics. As a result, adults and young people rarely 'learn' together.
- Outside school there are few contexts in which young people can choose to listen to the voice of adults, or in which adults can listen to them. Mobile phones, the internet and television mean young people spend less time listening to adults and more time listening to their peers.
- When it comes to the generation gap, the questions raised by young people today seem so markedly different to the questions asked by previous

generations in their youth that adults often feel ill-equipped to communicate with them.
- There has been an overall parental and community disengagement from the responsibilities of training young people and an increasing reliance on specialists, both at school and within the church.

Twenty-first-century western culture also provides its own challenges. 'Culture is the ensemble of stories we tell each other,' wrote the social scientist Clifford Geertz. Communities throughout the ages have thrived by virtue of their ability to participate in, and listen to, shared stories. Today there are myriad stories to choose from but very few that bind us together as they did in the past. This 'atomisation' is a feature of UK culture in the period since the Second World War, accelerated by the multiplication of communication technologies, in particular television. The net impact on the formation and growth of youth culture and the resulting generation divide cannot be underestimated.

The rise of youth culture is inextricably linked with the growth of pop culture, which has provided different generations and youth subcultures with alternative pictures of what life should be like for a young person. So, for example, think of Elvis on a programme like the Ed Sullivan show. There are shots of Elvis and then a camera cut – not to a disapproving or indifferent adult in the TV audience but to a screaming teenage girl.[1] So teenage girls the world over knew exactly how they were supposed to respond to icons like Elvis – with fanatical devotion. This is just one of the factors that prised young people away from seeing normal adults as role models and that have helped 'youth' create its own story.

Young people's decisions to listen to pop stars rather than parents are one factor in the process by which family loyalties and ties have been usurped by powerful peer group affiliations. But more than that, our contemporary culture has shifted its focus from heroes to superstars. Rather than honouring those who seek to 'do what is right', who are attempting to make a contribution to a community, a movement, a nation or indeed the life of another human being, our young people have been increasingly hijacked by a celebrity culture. No wonder the vocational aims of young people today have tended to shift from traditional careers or following in parents' footsteps to desiring to imitate the latest teen icon.

The rise of the youth worker

With such cultural chaos and shifts in attitudes it's unsurprising that the church responded to the communication gap between generations by employing specialists who could speak a language that was fast becoming incomprehensible to many – the 'language' of youth. The youth worker was an answer to a gnawing question about the future of the church: 'How do we reach and keep young people?' But whilst youth work does provide a vital input amongst young people, in some respects it serves to separate children further from the adult population. Of course the young people come into contact with adult leaders within youth groups, but do those youth groups model in any way what happens in 'adult' society or church? Creating separate worlds for children, young people and adults is a trend firmly established in today's industrialised societies. The worlds of the computer game, the mobile phone and the internet all provide distinct spheres for children, which adult influence rarely impinges upon. On the whole, youth work has done exactly the same within the church.

Insulated childhood

One of the changes over the course of the nineteenth and twentieth centuries that have deeply impacted generational relations concerns how adult/child time is regulated and spent. As history professor John Gillis comments, 'Children's spaces are increasingly "islanded", separated from one another and from the adult world. Many childhoods are insulated from the adult world.'[2] In pre-industrial societies children would be in contact with adults in work and in worship. So, for example, either children would be working alongside adults or the homestead itself was the place where adults worked.

Today, workplace and home remain largely separate. We're also aware of both parents spending more time away from home at work. Because time at home or with children is limited, it is often not adult-focused but child-focused. Activities tend to be centred on children's timetables. Saturdays are filled with taking children to football practice or dance classes, or simply doing things that kids want to do – cinema, McDonalds, theme parks or playgrounds. As a result, when children spend time with adults they do not enter the adult world but a world constructed for their benefit by adults. The term 'quality time' often means time when parents serve the expectations of children, motivated sometimes by guilt arising from work life demands or marital separation, sometimes by a recognition of the important role that parents play in child development. But obviously this impacts how adults model adulthood to children.

One of the results of a 'kidicentric' culture is that contemporary families have an inability to build up resilience within children. Every need of the child is catered for. Children are not expected to perform tasks around the house, and so they do not learn that goals are accomplished through sacrifice or that their every whim cannot be satisfied. Modern families seem in danger of cocooning their young from certain forms of hardship, so that the children end up learning plenty about dependence and nothing about interdependence.

It's also been suggested that such factors could contribute to the increasing rates of depression and self-harm amongst teenagers. When teenagers are confronted with an emotional crisis and things do not go their way, they simply don't have the resilience or the coping mechanisms to deal with it. Relationship breakdowns or career disappointments produce emotional distress, which can lead to experimentation with drug abuse or self-harm.

The way ahead for discipling young people

So what are the implications of these factors for discipling young people? In one sense it's simply a question of understanding that disciple-making happens best in the context of role-modelling. Children learn how to act in the world from seeing how adults act. So in a world where the boundaries between childhood and adulthood are blurred, a simple solution is that adults need to *be* adults. When it comes to understanding what it means to be a mature follower of Christ, children look to adults, all the adults within the congregation of a church, not just the youth worker, not just the minister, not just the parents. We represent the journey's end as far as children are concerned.

So do we employ a youth worker who is charismatic, energetic and into the latest form of youth culture, be it PlayStation, Dance Mat or skateboarding? Or do we employ someone who isn't exactly like our young people – a mature Christian who leads by example, can build relationships and pass on biblical wisdom to our youth? Can we build churches that celebrate the communal role and responsibility of bringing up children in Christ?

Of course it's true that effective discipling begins at home. And when looking for biblical insight on parenting, people often turn to the Bible's book of Proverbs. This book exemplifies the role of elders in passing down wisdom to the young.

However, we may find Proverbs' attitude to parenting extreme: 'Spare the rod and spoil the child' isn't likely to go down well with a contemporary readership. But, as theologian Derek Kidner notes, Proverbs advocates the harsh disciplining of a child for two reasons. The first, as 22:15 illuminates, is that 'foolishness is bound up in the heart of a child', and so, as Kidner adds, 'it will take more than words to dislodge it'.[3] And the second imperative is that 'character (in which wisdom embodies itself) is a plant that grows more sturdily for some cutting back'.[4] As 29:15 states, a child left to its own devices will only produce shame for the parent.

This stance – that the adult often knows what is good for the child – has been undermined in today's world, but not entirely eradicated. For instance, children may think they or their peers know better when it comes to relationships or fashion, but we do draw the line at allowing children to provide their own syllabus for GCSE – or to eat fast food all the time.

In the church, we've perhaps negotiated too much with children. We pander to what we believe are the needs of children to the extent that the role of adults is diminished. Or perhaps it's the case that adults within the church have themselves been over-dependent on passive models of biblical teaching and are now ill-equipped to engage with young people's questions of faith. Indeed, adults sometimes have little resilience of their own when it comes to facing the difficult choices that faith asks them to make.

The purpose of looking briefly at Proverbs is not to advocate the wide-scale reintroduction of the slipper but to highlight the biblical emphasis on the important role of elders in bringing up children. If the church is haemorrhaging teenagers, we have to ask ourselves if it is because we address the issue of discipleship too late. The spiritual education we provide for our young people is neither consistent enough nor rigorous enough to equip them with a strong and stable faith in a time when there are many challenges to the authenticity and relevance of our beliefs.

Deuteronomy 6 emphasises the communal aspect of introducing faith to the young. The *shema*, the divine imperative central to our faith, 'love the Lord your God with all your heart, and with all your soul, and with all your might,' is followed by another instruction: 'Keep these words that I am commanding you today in your heart. Recite them to your children and talk about them when you are at home and when you are away, when you lie down and when you rise.' It is vital that we embrace a vision of disciple-making that is holistic, encompassing every area of life. Celebrating faith in the home is an essential aspect of this, and a wealth of resources aimed at encouraging teaching in the home is available.[5]

Discipling our young people is obviously an essential part of shaping the future of the church. The most important thing in encouraging them to develop a well-rounded and vital understanding of what it means to follow Christ is to have that passion for following Christ ourselves. It's a passion that actively seeks to create communities not of convenience but of sacrifice, giving up time and energy to aid the training of young people in the church. We need to generate discussion about faith whenever we can: at home, at the meal table, in the car, in the nursery.

Conclusion

As the incident in the temple illustrated, it is important that we provide a context in which young people can ask questions about faith and learn not just from the youth worker or pastor but from the whole congregation. To what extent does the adult learning and teaching in our churches model how to do that? Is there a context for questioning and discussion? Is just one voice heard expressing biblical wisdom? Do we address the difficult faith questions presented in the twenty-first century? Our young people are growing up in a society where there is a proliferation of worldviews. Questions about the uniqueness of Christ and the authenticity of the Bible, as well as serious thinking about moral and ethical dilemmas, all need to be wrestled with within our churches. Perhaps when it comes to teaching children (and adults) we need to take off the kid gloves.

♦ ♦ ♦ ♦

Ten ideas for encouraging the discipling of young people in the church

1. Encourage maturity by giving children from ten upwards 'responsible' roles in church services: welcoming on the door, delivering the Bible reading, creating church notices on PowerPoint to loop before the service.
2. Many parents read the Bible to their children, but how many children actually see their parents reading the Bible and praying, or are aware of parents having quiet times? Role-modelling matters.
3. Remember home is as much church as a Sunday morning service is. Celebrate faith actively midweek – e.g. family prayer times around the meal table, and celebrating the Christian calendar through creative crafts. (For ideas, see *Feast of Faith: Celebrating the Christian Year at Home* by Kevin and Stephanie Parkes, Church House Publishing 2000.)
4. Encourage more cross-generational learning. For example, get the whole church family together to do a 'Walk Thru the Bible' session – a fun way of learning Bible history (www.bible.org.uk).
5. Link in to *essential*, the Evangelical Alliance's new youth theology project, which details resources to help young people think deeper about their faith (www.eauk.org).
6. If we expect teenagers to sit through sermons, get the preacher to provide a handout they can follow and fill in, e.g. questions they can answer: 'What does worship mean?' etc.
7. In order for adults to 'share' biblical wisdom, they need to have some in the first place! Many churches are conducting evening-school lessons for congregation members, e.g. modules on church

history, how to preach, introduction to the New Testament. Is yours?

8. Teaching our young people about faith is often approached from an 'issues' starting point, e.g. start with sex and relationships and then make a link to the Bible – Adam and Eve. Why not do it the other way round? One church in North Lancashire has created a cell group curriculum for their young people that means if they stay with the church from 11 to 18 they'll have covered every book in the Bible. They look at the issues raised by each book as they go along.
9. Relate biblical truth to cultural topics. If you make it your church's practice to think about issues such as the media from a Christian perspective, for example by having sermons that address television and the internet, then when young people are engaging with those media midweek it might just inspire them to think about faith!
10. One church on the south coast experimented with inter-generational cell groups – two or three adults and around five young people. They didn't get together midweek but met during the sermon on a Sunday morning for a ten-week period. They looked at a particular book of the Bible and then presented their findings as groups to the rest of the congregation at the end of the course.

Further reading

Brown, B.Bradford, Reed W. Larson and T.S. Saraswathi (eds.), *The World's Youth* (Cambridge University Press, 2002)

Bunge, Marcia J. (ed.), *The Child in Christian Thought*, (Wm. B. Eerdmans Publishing Co., 2001)

Gillis, John R., 'Childhood and Family Time' in An-Magritt Jensen and Lorna McKee (eds.), *Children and the Changing Family: Between Transformation and Negotiation* (Routledge Falmer, 2003)

Strommen, Merton P. and Richard A. Hardel, *Passing on the Faith: a Radical New Model for Youth and Family Ministry* (St Mary's Press, 2000)

Withers, Margaret, *Mission-shaped Children: Moving Towards a Child-centered Church* (Church House Publishing, 2006)

Notes

1 Andy Bennett, *Cultures of Popular Music* (Open University Press, 2001).

2 John R Gillis, 'Childhood and Family Time' in An-Magritt Jensen and Lorna McKee (eds.), *Children and the Changing Family: Between Transformation and Negotiation* (Routledge Falmer, 2003).

3 Derek Kidner, *Proverbs: an Introduction & Commentary* Tyndale Commentary (IVP, reprint 2003).

4 Ibid.

5 For example, Kevin and Stephanie Parkes, *Feast of Faith: Celebrating the Christian Year at Home* (Church House Publishing 2000); Merton P. Strommen and Richard A. Hardel, *Passing on the Faith: a Radical New Model for Youth and Family Ministry* (St. Mary's Press, 2000).

13

Learning to live: can adult education best practice contribute towards the making of Christian disciples?

Margaret Killingray

Margaret is a tutor at the London Institute for Contemporary Christianity (LICC), where she teaches on interpreting the Bible in today's world, specialising in ethics and relationships. She is also responsible for LICC's weekly Word for the Week *email service. Margaret has degrees in sociology and theology, and has been involved in adult learning and teaching for many years. She writes for the Bible Reading Fellowship's* Day by Day with God *Bible reading notes.*

In this chapter Margaret explores the ways in which our understanding of how adults learn could help us construct more effective models of disciple-making. She introduces some principles and practices of adult learning and teaching, outlines how adults learn best and highlights some implications of these for disciple-making today.

For reflection

- How could what you understand about adult learning impact how you seek to make disciples in your church?
- What could you do easily and simply to move forward?

Learning to live: can adult education best practice contribute towards the making of Christian disciples?

> His divine power has given us everything needed for life and godliness, through the knowledge of him who called us by his own glory and goodness ... For this very reason, you must make every effort to support your faith with goodness, and goodness with knowledge, and knowledge with self-control, and self-control with endurance, and endurance with godliness, and godliness with mutual affection, and mutual affection with love. For if these things are yours and are increasing among you, they keep you from being ineffective and unfruitful in the knowledge of our Lord Jesus Christ (2 Pet. 1:3-8).

As human beings we continue to 'learn' throughout our lives, learning – and forgetting – in myriad chaotic ways. All of us are in a process of day-by-day living and learning, but Christian adults also need to learn how to be disciples. New creations have to learn how to live in a new way. The process of becoming whole-life disciples raises all kinds of challenging issues. In this chapter I want to open a discussion on the ways in which our understanding of how adults learn could help us construct more effective models of disciple-making. I shall focus primarily on group learning, though I recognise this is only one dimension of a total approach to adult learning. And you may well wish to read this chapter in parallel with Jason Clark's material on adult learning in Chapter 14: What does disciple-making look like in the emerging church?

A syllabus for discipleship?

Discipleship involves learning. We need to grow in knowledge and understanding of our faith and its application to all areas of life in a growing relationship with the Lord, to the full extent of our gifts and abilities. What kinds of things should Christians be learning? The syllabus might include a growing understanding of the Bible; an ability to talk about one's faith, its doctrines and its history; an understanding of how one's church came to be and of broader ecclesiological differences. It might include the development of a Christian worldview so that one is able to assess critically all aspects of life and culture from a Christian perspective and develop an ability to make everyday ethical decisions based on Christian principles. It might include the development of faith skills that support a growing relationship with God – prayer, spiritual disciplines and so on. It might include learning about the character and purposes of our Triune God; our identity in Christ; the breadth of his glorious salvation through the cross; growing in our experience of God through his Spirit; becoming confident in the place we have in God's work on earth as well as the hope we have for our destiny. Many people put a great deal of effort into becoming adept in their areas of expertise – profession, home management, use of technology, social relationships and so on. The challenge is to know our faith and to live it as well as we can.

But discipleship involves growth in wisdom as well as knowledge.[1] A Spirit-led transformation of our minds and hearts involves an overturning and reassessing of all our previously held values, a radical re-evaluation of what it means to be human, 'successful', mature and good. We need to learn to be new counter-cultural creations.

A context for the disciple as an adult learner?

Christians have, of course, always been involved in learning their faith and developing as disciples in one way or another.[2] But the traditional Christendom model of belonging to the church from cradle to grave and the post-Reformation model of children growing up, learning their faith from church, home and school are, in the main, no longer valid. The decline in church attendance and in the numbers of children and young people in Sunday schools, as well as in Christian input within schools, has led to significant loss of a common knowledge of Christian ideas and stories. There is no longer a cultural underpinning of Christian belief and practice. This means that the planned and self-conscious education of new, and indeed not so new, Christians is a far more important process. To a certain degree we see this reflected in the growth of small groups within many church streams, in the development of national resources such as Alpha and Christianity Explored and so on. Sunday services, too, remain crucial for Christian learning, since surveys indicate that fewer Christians are doing any self-directed Bible reading and study, and few churches have more than a third of their membership involved in small groups. But in all these contexts, do we see the appropriate application of a growing body of theory and praxis from the world of adult education?

Biblical models of learning and teaching

The world of adult education has expanded over the past decades, at university level, in short courses of all kinds, and in local day and evening classes. This has led to a growing body of research and experience-led resources on adult education. This body of knowledge helps us to understand adults' preferred ways of learning and the teaching patterns that are most effective. Before looking at these, however, I would like to ask, very briefly, whether there are useful models of learning and teaching in the Bible.

In the Old Testament, teaching involves the wider community, and parents in particular play a significant role in teaching their children. There are many methods: allegories and parables, dramatic reconstructions, festivals in yearly cycles. The Israelites' history and experience of Yahweh – for example, through the exodus and the period of exile – are integrated into rituals and rhythms of life that form part of the teaching process. New Testament patterns, particularly in the gospels, include apprenticeship, parable, open-ended questioning, practical demonstration, reflection on experience, and telling and retelling. The main thrust of the biblical concepts of maturing and learning is that they take place within the relational networks of a Christian community. In the New Testament, Christian learning took place in homes and fellowships where Christians shared and all contributed, where teaching was a general ministry of all but the gift and special calling of some.

Furthermore the inherent nature of the Bible is informative. Since the Bible is a primary vehicle for God's teaching, its startling variety of styles and types of speech and literature should suggest that our teaching could be equally varied. But a keynote throughout the Bible is that the end goal of all learning and teaching is wisdom and understanding, not merely the gaining of knowledge. Precepts and laws are to be obeyed with understanding and as an act of love. Doctrines are to be lived out.

Principles and practice of adult learning and teaching

Key elements of learning include understanding, reflection, memory and action. First we hear or see, then we take in and understand, then we remember and finally we do something about it, taking action or changing our behaviour and attitudes. No one of these should be emphasised at the expense of the others. We are presented with learning experiences all our lives. These include both formal (reading the paper, going on a college course, learning to use a new computer application, watching television or going to church) and informal (having an accident, walking in the woods, having a baby, a sudden inspiration, arguing with a partner) experiences. Experience then involves some *reflection,* in that our attention is focused at some level. Repeated exposure to similar experiences becomes part of our *conditioning,* usually without our being aware of it. These last two processes then build our *worldview,* our conceptual understanding of our world and ourselves. On the basis of these we then live, behave and act. We can see that Christian conversion should be the kind of experience that begins a process of radical change and re-formation at every point in this process. We want to make disciples whose learning experiences, reflection, concept formation and action become more Christlike as they grow into Christian maturity.

Two accusations

Before looking at the practical detail of adult learning, there are two accusations that have been aimed at faith-based Christian teaching. Firstly, that it involves indoctrination and sometimes brainwashing. Secondly, that it encourages dependency and reinforces class and social elitism and authoritarian structures.

Is Christian teaching indoctrination by definition? Religion, politics and morality were all areas where indoctrination by teachers was feared, particularly during the social changes of the 1960s. Liberal educators assumed that science and maths were not a problem because they contained no 'doctrines', only ascertainable facts. Although this kind of argument has largely been discredited, it is obviously possible for teachers, particularly where there is no external accountability, to use their position of status and authority to indoctrinate. The fear of indoctrination is aroused not just by content, but also by teaching methods, teachers' motives and intentions and the possible consequence of closed minds and antipathy to any other views. We know that this does happen, particularly in some parts of the church. Respect for the autonomy of the individual and a willingness to encourage an openness that is able to question one's own beliefs are seen as crucial aspects of liberal education.

As for the second charge, writers such as Paulo Freire[3] argued in the 1970s for empowering the disadvantaged by encouraging them to take charge of their own lives and learning. Liberation theology challenged orthodox mainstream Christians to be practitioners as well as theoreticians. Such radical theology encouraged adult educators to understand adult learning as empowering new Christians to be agents of change for themselves, for others and for the world. Educationally, such empowering used a hermeneutic of praxis, whereby action and experience led to reflection and reassessment and then on to fresh action. Seeing God as the driving force of history, passionately involved in the world, led to passionate engagement. Christians were not to be pietistic and passive, but enabled to confront, act and engage.

How then do adults learn best?

What are the best practices for setting up structured, planned group-learning programmes? When adults join groups to learn something, they bring with them their previous learning experiences, including school ones. They come on a voluntary basis, and may not like being told what to do and when to do it, in a way that recalls past schoolrooms. In secondary and tertiary education there is a strong sense of pressure to perform well, to compete and to do better. This can leave some with a sense of failure, a lack of confidence, an underestimation of ability and a fear of displaying ignorance. These observations lead to some helpful guidelines for effective adult learning.

Adult learning should incorporate the experience adults have already gained, without undervaluing or overvaluing such contributions. Some already acquired knowledge may have to be unlearned. Adults have already learned a lot by doing, gaining implicit theory drawn from practice, through trial, error and success. They should be encouraged to contribute from this resource, though also to recognise the problems that can arise when personal experience is used to make generalisations.

Adult learning should involve participation and mutual encouragement. This includes the monitoring and evaluating of learning by individuals, of themselves, each other and their 'tutors'. It also includes mutual nurturing and pastoring and, with 'tutor' help, the setting of realistic goals and constructive feedback.

Adult learning involves self-direction, including negotiation over syllabus and teaching methods. Adults should develop self-criticism, the ability to evaluate and analyse skills, knowledge, behaviour and attitudes. They should be encouraged to be aware of their own learning and monitor how successful they are. Their expectations need to be expressed so that the group can work out whether they can reasonably be met.

Adult learning involves the use of a wide range of resources, including variety in ideas, content and materials and a variety of methods and approaches.

Adults have different preferred learning styles.[4] It is important to provide a range of learning opportunities to match the needs of different people. Many of us assume that others will be as comfortable as we are with our own preferred learning style. In fact what helped us may not be the best or only way for others. The Honey and Mumford questionnaire[5] seeks to identify the relative strengths of four different types of learner – activists, reflectors, theorists and pragmatists. Like another personality indicator, Myers-Briggs, this questionnaire helps both students and teachers to understand why different people prefer to learn in different ways. A rather simple summary is: *activists* learn best when there is challenge; *reflectors* when they are given time and space to stand back; *theorists* when they can listen to or read ideas that are logical; and *pragmatists* when they are working on something they can try out in practice.

The role of the teacher with adult learners

The 'teacher' may take on various roles according to the kind of teaching that is required. They may be a transmitter of information, logically and reasonably. They may be an enabler and facilitator aiming to bring about individual and social change, empowering adults to make judgements and to act. They may be a pastor and counsellor, allowing space for creativity, finding meaning in adults' words and actions. They may be an instructor who solves technical problems and promotes competence, efficiency and productivity. They may be a preacher, proclaiming the truth.

An experienced teacher of adults works to the aims of the group but allows other aims, often unplanned, to be verbalised and worked through. They are able to deal with disagreement and conflict and are willing to allow a different conclusion to emerge from the one they planned. The teacher will model the wise handling of individuals; will help people take part, hearing the muttered comment; will notice the disgruntled and puzzled; will protect participants from embarrassment or ridicule.

Implications for disciple-making

These guidelines point to smallish interactive groups as often being the best place for adults to learn. This is not always what people actually say they prefer. Many imply that they don't want to make this kind of effort and would prefer to sit and listen. (A weekly quiz on the sermon may convince them that some other input is needed!) They also point to the need for a system of training in which teachers and group leaders learn how to facilitate good practice.

There are, however, some other aspects of Christian adult learning. All Christian teaching is teaching for commitment, both for initial conversion and for a continuing life of obedience. But we do not need to draw strict lines between these two. We know that people become Christians at different stages and in different ways. Some may come slowly to faith in a mature Christian group, hearing the call to faith when discussing issues of discipleship. In church learning, the long-term relationships of those who belong to the same fellowship can create a different dynamic from short-term courses taught to strangers. The role of prayer, particularly when personal lifestyle and relationships are being examined, may be very important. There may be times when confession and repentance are appropriate.

Conclusion

I am aware that there are many questions I haven't begun to address in this short chapter. How far should boundaries of orthodoxy be put on learning? Should teachers be prepared to stop those who might mislead and worry weaker students? Or should the aim be to enable adults to sift, judge and assess good and not so good contributions, as risk-takers and boundary-pushers? Some have argued that the Holy Spirit works in special and transcendental ways in conversion and sanctification and that the emphasis should be on waiting for the Spirit to transform our minds rather than on working to earn new knowledge. Can we best talk about Christian learning in theological terms or educational? Does God transcend normal human processes of learning, whether in a small group or listening to a sermon?

What I hope that I have done, however, is open a discussion about how we might optimise what we now know about adult learning in the contexts in which we're trying to help adults learn what it means to be a follower of Jesus. Some guidelines are easily adaptable to a disciple-making context. Others have more complex ramifications. What is clear, though, is that the quality of relationships within a disciple-making community is a primary factor in effective growth in faith and life. Centuries of Christian disciple-making have shown the value of some kind of personal accountability to another, either by established patterns of spiritual direction or through less formal links. The aim is that all disciples are part of a dynamic, intentional relationship of trust in which one person enables another to maximise the grace of God in their lives by sharing their life, experiences and resources. This pattern of apprenticeship occurs in so many forms in the Bible: Jesus and the disciples; Paul and his co-travellers; the patterns of training underpinning the letters to Titus and Timothy. However far we feel we still have to go in applying some principles of adult learning to the challenge of helping adults mature in faith and life, we can each start with one other. Could you make yourself accountable to another Christian or be such a friend to a fellow disciple, so that together you might know Christ better and make him known?

> This is the covenant that I will make with the house of Israel after those days, says the Lord: I will put my laws in their minds, and write them on their hearts, and I will be their God, and they shall be my people. And they shall not teach one another or say to one another, 'Know the Lord,' for they shall all know me, from the least of them to the greatest (Heb. 8:10-11, quoting Jer. 31:33-34).

♦ ♦ ♦ ♦

Further reading

Ballard, Paul and John Pritchard, *Practical Theology in Action* (SPCK, 1996)

Craig, Yvonne, *Learning for life: a Handbook of Adult Religious Education* (Mowbray, 1994, reprint 2003 unrevised)

Daines, John et al., *Adult Learning, Adult Teaching* (Welsh Academic Press, 2002)

Killingray, Margaret, *Encouraging Biblical Literacy*, Grove Booklet B6 (Grove, 1997)

Rogers, Alan, *Teaching Adults* (Open University Press, 2002)

Rogers, Jenny, *Adults Learning* (Open University Press, 2001)

Notes

1 See chapter 6: Shaping the disciple's mind.

2 See chapter 4: From darkness to light.

3 See Paulo Freire, *Pedagogy of the Oppressed*, (Penguin, 1996).

4 See chapter 14: What does disciple-making look like in the emerging church?

5 For detail see www.peterhoney.com/product/booklet

Learning from current practice

14

What does disciple-making look like in the emerging church?

Jason Clark

Jason took a degree in theology at London School of Theology in 1991, then qualified as a high school teacher. He was then an investment broker in the City of London for eight years. In 1997 he and his wife Bev planted an 'emerging church' linked to the Vineyard movement in Sutton, Surrey. Nearly two-thirds of the church community were previously unchurched, but today around two hundred adults and one hundred children are actively involved. They have recently planted another church. Jason has completed a part-time Doctor of Ministry degree in postmodern theology and leadership with Len Sweet, at George Fox University. He coordinates the UK activities of Emergent.

In this chapter Jason suggests that if the church is to facilitate the formation of disciples in our emerging culture we cannot rely on standard growth practices but must develop new ways of understanding and enabling growth. He focuses on the need for holistic strategies and unpacks some of the experiments he has been involved in with the church he's planted.

For reflection

- What do you think about how people grow?
- What might you experiment with in your context?

What does disciple-making look like in the emerging church?

What could be the impact of Christians in today's world if our churches provided space for spiritual development, offered authentic community and engaged creatively and sensitively with contemporary culture? As a leader in a church that would identify itself as part of the emerging church movement, I have wrestled both theologically and practically over a number of years with the question of disciple-making in our contemporary culture. The church plant that I have been involved with for nearly a decade has reflected and experimented extensively with different approaches to helping new Christians grow. In our particular church culture this has meant learning how we can engage new believers from primarily 'non-churched' backgrounds in a process of maturing in faith and life. How can we 'do life' together in ways that form us into an authentic, culturally engaged and kingdom-focused community? What sort of processes and methods best embody the reality of the living God for followers of Jesus in a postmodern, post-Christian, pluralistic culture? And importantly, how do we work all this out within the fabric of our everyday lives?

My thesis in this chapter is this: today's predominant church education methods are largely ineffective in forming disciples of Christ in our emerging culture, primarily because they do not embody a holistic approach to Christian growth. They are not able to engage the diverse ways in which human beings learn. They largely fail to tackle the realities of daily life. And they struggle to harness the breadth of human experience into the process of growth in ways that cohere with a deep need for authenticity. This is particularly true with regard to experiences of doubt and questioning. In this chapter I want to unpack this a little further and then present a selection of our experiments towards a more holistic approach to Christian growth.

I should make two points at the outset. The title of this chapter, with its 'emerging church' nomenclature, is somewhat dangerous since it opens up too many interesting avenues of exploration that are obviously beyond the scope of a study such as this. The focus here is not the 'emerging church' per se. Rather I aim to describe something of our experience as a church living in an emerging postmodern culture amongst certain types of people for whom a holistic growth strategy is proving to be absolutely crucial. Which leads to my second point. I identify not only with the emerging church movement but also with all churches that are working to make disciples of Jesus Christ in today's world. I trust therefore that our experiences, limited indeed as they are, will generate new conversations and stimulate imaginative possibilities in a wide variety of church cultures.

What does healthy growth look like?

In his letter to the Ephesians Paul exhorts Christians to 'grow up in every way into him who is the head, into Christ' (Eph. 4:15). How then do we grow? How do we participate in a process that leads towards our transformation into Christlikeness? In the words of James Fowler, 'How do we recognise some of the patterns of struggle, growth, and change that characterise human beings in the process of becoming aware, conscious, and increasingly responsive and responsible selves, as partners with God?'[1] I want to suggest that most of today's standard growth practices have two inherent weaknesses that are now limiting growth in a postmodern context. I'll explore this a little further before looking at ways we have attempted to tackle them.

Current models: the weaknesses of cognition and socialisation

Brett Webb-Mitchell, an American pastor, scholar and practitioner of Christian education, provides an overview of the modern church growth process in his book *Christly Gestures*.[2] In it he concludes that the growth process is predicated on two core models: one of cognitive learning and a social model of education understood as 'education-as-entertainment'. The former funnels the growth process into one narrow dimension, and the latter supports a consumerist approach to Christian growth based on 'what is most pleasing, emotionally speaking, to the Learner'. The net result of both models is selfish learning, where enlightenment of the mind is the goal of growth and Christians are unable to develop patterns of life that are connected to each other and to the world around them.[3]

Furthermore, as James Fowler suggests in his research, a normal and vital part of Christian growth is the process of wrestling with doubts and questions. Cognitive learning systems, however, are often used to teach certainty. Consequently they risk squeezing out other mechanisms that might also promote growth. Christians often respond in two ways when what they are supposed to believe doesn't hold up in their everyday life. Some compartmentalise their lives, with their church or faith life occupying one area and work, school and so on occupying another – the classic sacred-secular divide. Many others faced with this breakdown leave the church.[4]

Towards a habitat for disciple-making

What, then, are some of the metaphors that might help us think beyond the limitations of these present models for disciple-making? There are two that are particularly apt for our contemporary context. First, there is the metaphor of 'habitat'. Present models of disciple-making often have more than a passing resemblance to programming a machine in order to produce certain outcomes. Approaching the challenge as the creation of certain kinds of 'habitat' that are conducive to growth and development for Christians can open up new possibilities.[5]

Then there is the metaphor of a web. The current modern church system of growth can be likened to building a wall of knowledge. For a postmodern context a better metaphor might be a web. A web has nodes of connection. Growth takes place by movement between nodes, and nodes have multiple connections to one another. They are not foundational like a wall. A wall is monolithic; it is about certainty and non-movement. A web allows multiple places to locate, and is able to flex and move. So instead of a typical ten-week discipleship course based around cognitive learning, we might provide a variety of 'nodes' to which people would connect. These might include intentional learning courses/spaces, as well as more spontaneous relational places for food, for 'doing life' together.

Holistic strategies for disciple-making

Whatever metaphors ultimately prove to be most helpful for postmodern people, the goal is one of whole-life disciple-making. Today's culture is increasingly looking for 'things that work'. A holistic learning process is essential for disciples of Christ who are learning to live authentic and integrated lives that also connect to the people, issues and challenges of today's world. Our church has tried to embrace a holistic discipling process that goes beyond the cognitive, and instead includes discussion and learning, and encourages people in the process of questioning and forming their beliefs. Along the way we have discovered that certain frameworks helpfully shape this process. I'd like to highlight four in particular.

1. *Psychodynamics*
   Growth is shaped by many factors, and these include the diversity of being human. Knowing oneself can play a dynamic role. Psychodynamic tools such as the Myers-Briggs Type Indicator,[6] the Enneagram,[7] DISC test,[8] or guided work with a trained professional can be used to help people develop self-awareness that can then be applied to the learning process.

2. *Socialisation*
   It is vital that people who wish to grow form supportive relationships with others who are also seeking growth. Rodney Clapp has asserted that Christians cannot grow unless they are supported by the subculture they inhabit.[9]

3. *Doubt-questioning*
   Alan Jamieson suggests that growth includes bringing people to see doubt and uncertainty as a vital part of their growth.[10] The structure of the modern church fails to allow these elements to contribute towards growth. Instead, certainty is

espoused as a sign of faith and maturity.[11] We must move our churches to be places where doubt, mystery, pain and uncertainty are normal places for growth and exploration, not things to avoid or to deny.

4. *Preferred learning styles*

People learn in different ways, and we sometimes talk about visual, verbal or kinaesthetic learning styles.[12] But learning styles can be expressed in many ways. In particular we have found it helpful to pay attention to:

Space

Joe Myers in *The Search to Belong*[13] has shown that people connect, belong and form relationships in four key spaces – public, social, private and intimate. It has been a helpful matrix for us when trying to provide a range of contexts to facilitate deeper relationships.

Media

Media are the means by which we might channel teaching and could include classroom-type teaching but also books, one-to-one coaching, mentoring, listening and physical movement. We have explored a variety of these.

Time

We live in a culture that is confronted with so many options and choices and is often poor in its management of time. Helping each other to understand time, not only time management[14] but also the nature and spirituality of time, can open up new avenues for effective learning.[15]

From theory to praxis

The process of understanding the weaknesses inherent in current models of disciple-making, exploring new approaches to the formation of Christian disciples and developing certain frameworks that might shape those approaches has been one of experimentation and reflection over several years. I'd like to share some examples of what this experimentation has looked like in our church plant.

Journey

'Journey' was an intentional discussion group for Christians and people wanting to find out about the Christian faith. Rather than using a cognitive approach such as Alpha, we developed an approach based on the idea of *Socrates' Café*,[16] allowing people to ask questions and offer answers themselves. Approximately fifty people met in the function room of a pub for one night several weeks running. At the start of one evening, we put people into groups of ten and asked each group to come up with the most difficult questions they could think of about Christianity. Then, rather than offer the 'correct' answers, we asked each group to take one question and try to answer it themselves. My role was to act as a commentator, offering input from Christian history and doctrine. At no time did I assert 'you must believe this' or 'this is the truth' but rather I offered multiple answers that the church might have and the one I was most comfortable with.

DISC – elders' retreat

Our eldership team spent a weekend away together that included a day looking at how we might understand one another better and deal with conflict more effectively as a team. This was facilitated by a consultant who used the DISC analysis with us in order to help us recognise our diversity as a team and to learn how to harness that diversity to better handle the issues we faced. This was a good example of growing in emotional maturity.

Red button
This eight-week course was based largely on Daniel Goleman's premise in *Emotional Intelligence*.[17] It focused on various aspects of emotional intelligence, including anger, grief, boundaries, transactional analysis and life stages. Most of the evening was spent receiving input from a trainer and the rest in interactive work on issues with which people were struggling.

EPIC
Using the idea of EPIC (Experiential, Participatory, Image Driven, and Connected) from Len Sweet,[18] we have modified our Sunday service considerably. We now have a media-arts team that produces video, reflections, interactions and activities around the theme we are exploring each Sunday. My talks have changed to a more interactive approach whereby I act as commentator and facilitator as we read a passage together and ask people to share what they think, see and hear in the passage. I summarise, provide commentary and suggest application.

God@Work
We started a group for people who want to explore how they can develop their faith at work, looking at what they are called to, what they are good at, and how they can have impact at work, support their colleagues and help their companies.

Creative arts
We have gathered a group of people from our church community who are exploring the creative arts – everything from understanding the spirituality of their interests to training and developing their skills, together with its application to their lives, our community and our church. Our hope is that our church will be known as a place to connect with and explore the creative and artistic.

Hospitality and discussion
We have existing small groups composed of people of different ages in multiple locations who seek to meet weekly and who invite friends, neighbours and people new to our church into their community life. These groups focus on eating, relaxing together and talking honestly and openly about life. We have developed a culture where questions at the deepest and hardest level are safe to ask and even encouraged. These groups are intimate spaces that offer the chance to really know and be known.

Movie nights
We have a group that organises trips to the movies, or uses our church centre (a large room with sofas, coffee machine, video screen and projector) to watch films and then eat food and discuss them together. This is a chance to talk about life issues and to be honest, open and vulnerable. We have found that in an image-based society, movies open the doors for people to examine themselves and their beliefs in ways that are moving and exciting.

Socials
We have parties, discos, music nights, X-Box LAN games nights, potlucks, bowling matches, theatre nights. The idea is that we have people in our community 'doing life'

together and inviting their friends and family into those spaces. There is no desire to bait and switch, i.e. to use these places as traps and then share a propositional message. Rather they are space in which we encourage our church to have a fully orbed life that can naturally include their friends.

Rule of faith
Using the Benedictine Rule of Faith,[19] we have explored what it means for some of us in the church community to live a more intentional and disciplined life, with daily prayers, and living closer to each other. We are exploring the possibility of some of us living in community, creating a space for people to grow for short or longer periods. We have also found the Benedictine approach to faith and work very applicable to our lifestyles.

Community action
From the first days of the church, we have made involvement in our larger community something we expect everyone to participate in. This culminated in one hundred volunteers from the church taking on a developing project that serves several hundred families a year. It now has its own building and staff, and we are known locally as the church that engages with our community's issues.

Conclusion

In exploring what healthy Christian disciple-making for an emerging postmodern culture might look like, I have suggested that we need church to be a place where people face the real issues of their lives and faith in a learning context which supports a diversity of approaches, and in particular embraces uncertainty, fear and doubt, in order to grow deeper in faith and obedience to Christ. This is enormously demanding of a leadership team and indeed of the community of God's people. It requires significant levels of commitment to one another and a willingness to embark on a journey that is often painful and highly sacrificial.

But the prize is great. We want to be living integrated and authentic lives that point to the reality of our Creator God. We want to be the people we are destined to become in Christ. We want to engage meaningfully with the challenges of today's world so that we can make a difference wherever we are. We believe in the church and we are convinced that wonderful opportunities for growth exist if only we are willing to re-imagine disciple-making in our contemporary culture. So we continue to reflect and to experiment.

♦ ♦ ♦ ♦

Further reading

Cloud, Henry and John Sims Townsend, *How People Grow: What the Bible Reveals About Personal Growth* (Zondervan, 2001)

Fowler, James W., Karl Ernst Nipkow and Friedrich Schweitzer, *Stages of Faith and Religious Development: Implications for Church, Education, and Society* (Crossroad, 1991)

Pagitt, Doug, *Reimagining Spiritual Formation: A Week in the Life of an Experimental Church* (Zondervan, 2004)

Peterson, Eugene H., *A Long Obedience in the Same Direction: Discipleship in an Instant Society* (Marshall Pickering, 1989)

Riddell, Michael, *Threshold of the Future: Reforming the Church in the Post-Christian West* (SPCK, 1998)

Notes

1 James Fowler, *Faith Development and Pastoral Care* (Fortress Press, 1987).

2 Brett Webb-Mitchell, *Christly Gestures: Learning to Be Members of the Body of Christ* (Eerdmans, 2003).

3 Thom and Joani Schulz, *Why Nobody Learns Much of Anything at Church* (Group Publishing, 2004).

4 Alan Jamieson, *A Churchless Faith: Faith Journeys Beyond the Churches* (SPCK, 2002).

5 See Steven Johnson, *Emergence: The Connected Lives of Ants, Brains, Cities, and Software* (Scribner, 2001).

6 Naomi Quenk, *Essentials of Myers-Briggs Type Indicator Assessment* (J. Wiley & Sons, 2000).

7 Don Richard Riso and Russ Hudson, *The Wisdom of the Enneagram: The Complete Guide to Psychological and Spiritual Growth for the Nine Personality Types* (Bantam Books, 1999).

8 Mels Carbonell, *Uniquely You: Understanding Personalities from a Biblical Perspective* (Personality Wise Ministries, 1993).

9 Rodney Clapp, *A Peculiar People: The Church as Culture in a Post-Christian Society* (InterVarsity Press, 1996).

10 Alan Jamieson, *Journeying in Faith: In and Beyond the Tough Places* (SPCK, 2004).

11 Jeremy Young, *The Cost of Certainty: How Religious Conviction Betrays the Human Psyche* (Darton, Longman & Todd, 2004).

12 For example, an online test to identify preferences can be found at http://www.ldpride.net/learning_style.html

13 Joseph R. Myers, *The Search to Belong: Rethinking Intimacy, Community, and Small Groups* (Youth Specialties, 2003).

14 Stephen R. Covey, *The 7 Habits of Highly Effective Families: Building a Beautiful Family Culture in a Turbulent World* (Franklin Covey/Golden Books, 1997).

15 For the most amazing study on the nature and spirituality of time see Christine Aroney-Sine, *Sacred Rhythms: Finding a Peaceful Pace in a Hectic World* (Baker Books, 2003).

16 Christopher Phillips, *Socrates' Café: A Fresh Taste of Philosophy* (W.W. Norton, 2001).

17 Daniel Goleman, *Emotional Intelligence* (Bantam Books, 1995).

18 Leonard Sweet, *Post-Modern Pilgrims: First Century Passion for the 21st Century World* (Broadman & Holman, 2000).

19 Eric Dean, *Saint Benedict for the Laity* (Liturgical Press, 1989); Wil Derkse and Martin Kessler, *The Rule of Benedict for Beginners: Spirituality for Daily Life* (Liturgical Press, 2003).

15

Lessons from Cell

Laurence Singlehurst

Laurence has been with Youth With A Mission (YWAM) for nearly thirty years and is also Director of Cell UK Ministries. Laurence's particular focus is on understanding postmodern culture and how to evangelise and disciple in that context. He is also involved in equipping churches in how to reach their communities through network evangelism empowered by cell church structures.

In this chapter Laurence explores the cultural context in which Cell has sought to contextualise its evangelism and discipleship. He identifies the lessons the cell movement has been learning through the cell church model about how to help Christians deepen and mature in their discipleship in the light of mission in the UK today.

For reflection

- What barriers to discipleship particularly resonate with you in this chapter?
- Does your context have certain DNA that you need to protect in order to encourage healthy growth in life and faith and mission?

Lessons from Cell

What have we learned through the cell movement about discipleship and evangelism in the last ten years? As I reflect on this question, I must begin by reminding us of the context in which we have been working in the past decade, in particular some significant factors arising from the shift from a modern to a postmodern worldview.

Firstly, as the power of the meta-narrative fades and cynicism towards claims for 'absolute truth' grows, proclamation evangelism has struggled. Concomitantly the idea of 'process' or 'journey' has become increasingly important in evangelism. People are on a journey of faith during which significant relationships with Christians who are living out their faith in an authentic way can have a major influence. Secondly, as Christian values have slowly receded from all spheres of life – business, the arts and so on – the need for the church to engage the public sphere with a Christian worldview that connects to the issues of our culture is increasingly urgent. These two dynamics – the personal and the public – both lead to the same conclusion: we have an urgent need for the whole body of Christ to live effectively as 'full-time Christian workers'. We need Christians who realise that God has called them to live his abundant life amongst the places and people that form their everyday context. We need to mobilise the whole body of Christ, equipping and releasing people to be God's instruments of transformation throughout our nation today.

But the prevailing culture has inevitably penetrated the church as well. A decline in Christian values in the world is reflected to varying degrees within the church, leading to significant discipleship issues. So we have young people who are enthusiastically dualist. They behave one way in their youth group and in a totally different way when out with their friends. They have the capacity to live in their Christian world and their non-Christian world with a greatly lowered conscience, seriously jeopardising the authenticity of their witness.

Within the adult church, too, there is a growing dualism. The gap between a Christian value system and the value system in the UK today is widening. In order to live counter-culturally Christians need more than a form of discipleship that just tells them what to do or not do. They need a way of living Christianly that works.[1]

In the light of all this, what has the UK cell movement learned?[2]

Lessons in evangelism

The cell model

Cell church has promoted a model of evangelism that is about love and relationships. We love people, and we build relationships with them. We create communities of Christians who meet in a small group, a cell, on a weekly basis, where they inspire one another to love God, to really love one another and to love their lost world – both the people they meet and the institutions they can influence. The cell movement has sought to embody relational evangelism. An important part of this has been an awareness of the significance of the workplace, and we have tried to make workplace mission foundational to these groups. The cell seeks to empower people to have an *oikos*, or network of relationships. The cell empowers them to be with these people as much as possible and to bring them into the cell community. These friends may not necessarily come to the cell meeting, but they are involved in the life of the cell – social gatherings and 'doing life' together. This way everybody gets to know each other's non-Christian friends, relationships are formed and a process begins. So the cell serves its members by supporting one another's friendships. The wider community, of which the cell group is a part – usually some form of larger Sunday celebration – serves the cell through the Sunday meetings and through Alpha-type courses. In this way there are both relationships and structures that we trust will help non-Christians on a journey towards commitment and integration into the body of Christ.

Lessons learned

We have learned that this is much harder to do in practice than in theory! Many people are very caught up in their relationship with God and their Christian community, and it is a challenge for everyone to become outward-focused. We have discovered that it takes a newly established cell church between two and five years, or even longer, to become outward-focused, to get to the stage where it is the norm for people to be in significant relationships with non-Christians, and for those to be intentional relationships of Christian love and truth. We have also learned that revival fantasy is still locked up in our souls. We hold on to a model of evangelism in which God will do everything and we (hopefully) will have to do nothing. At worst, we still believe deep down that evangelism is the responsibility of the leader and the evangelist.

For evangelism to become the passion and responsibility of every church member is a necessary but difficult journey. It is easy for cell groups to revert to being 'fellowship groups' unless there is something built into the group that gives it a clear focus. We have therefore learned that each cell needs to have a certain

DNA in order to keep a clear focus. This DNA has three strands drawn from the Great Commandment and the Great Commission: (1) we should love God and know his love for us; (2) we should sacrificially love the Christians around us; and (3) we should love the lost world in the widest sense, both relationally in seeking to win people, and also transformationally in terms of being salt and light. If you revert to just being a fellowship group where you might love God and love one another, there is nothing wrong with this, but it is not enough. To be a cell, there must be that third strand of loving our world. So we have learned that every dynamic small group needs a supervisor, someone who will visit that group once a month, who is a coach to the cell leader, who has the DNA of cell in their hearts and minds and who can coach that group on the journey to becoming a dynamic cell.

We've also learned that if you are going to train people to be cell leaders, it is not enough to give them the theory of cell, but they must personally experience it in a prototype model. If they just learn the theory in a seminar, under pressure they will revert to whatever model is in their subconscious; the experience of being part of a good prototype group before leading their own group changes that subconscious model to some extent.

More recently we have realised that for many of us, our approach to evangelism is still very mechanical. We are teaching methodologies, but not asking the questions 'Do we as Christians have love in our hearts for the world and the people in it? Do we really care? Do we share God's love for his world?' We must embrace these attitudes. Otherwise, all our systems are merely pressurising people.

Lessons from the workplace

Though we witness the seepage of Christian values out of society and a growing cynicism towards truth, people are nevertheless searching for authenticity. They're looking for integrity between the values people hold and the way they're lived out on a daily basis. Authentic people are attractive people. Where do many Christians get the opportunity to live out their discipleship in front of non-Christians? In the workplace. We have to slowly mobilise the body of Christ to be salt and light wherever they are Monday to Friday. We have to see this as a mission field and also as a context for our discipleship. Certainly it's a place where we try to live out Christian values. But more than that, it's also where we demonstrate what we really believe about human beings: that all people are made in the image of God. It's where our whole approach to life says something about who we believe God is. So, for example, God is a worker God. Work has inherent value to him. Viewed from this perspective the workplace becomes a highly significant context where our theology can be worked out in practice. So the cell movement has tried to create a vision for the workplace and to learn from people like Robert Warren,[3] Mark Greene[4] and many others. We have learned that cell churches need to create their vision for mission around the business of the people of the church, around what God has called them to do day by day.

Lessons in discipleship

The cell model

The cell model of discipleship is founded on two principles. Firstly, for real learning to take place, that is learning that prompts a change in thinking or behaviour, the teaching process must somewhere include facilitated discussion.[5] Through this facilitated discussion, ideas that are aired in big meetings and developed in coaching sessions later become reality in the context of small groups. These small groups become a place of mutual accountability to ensure that the theory is applied. So the cell movement takes the same view that John Wesley took: big meetings are very important; one-to-one conversations and discussions are important; but something very special happens in small groups through mutual accountability.

Discipleship involves changing people's belief and value systems. So the second principle of discipleship within the cell movement is that real discipleship has to be voluntary and not imposed; it must be something that people have a personal vision for that is then facilitated by the church; and worked out by the Holy Spirit.

Lessons learned

So what else have we learned on this journey? As has been seen in Alpha small groups, there is a real hunger in people to hear the sound of their own voices! Historically, a house group leader would have done perhaps 70 per cent of the talking in a weekly meeting. Retraining leaders to be facilitators, so that it is predominantly the voices of the group members that are heard, has been challenging, though not as difficult as some of the challenges we have faced in evangelism. This is simply because this interactive style of learning is a familiar part of today's culture in our schools and workplaces.

However, we also know that honesty is required to make these small groups work. Since discipleship has to do with real life and is not just about ideas, there has to be a measure of honesty as people share the problems they face in their lives for counsel and for prayer. The Holy Spirit is at work, and the group supports one another through their life-changing experiences. Though facilitated learning is part of our culture, honesty and vulnerability are not. Groups can adopt these values in theory, but it is much more challenging to put them into practice. Once again we see the importance of coaches who visit groups on a regular basis, and well-trained cell leaders who are able to model honesty and vulnerability so these characteristics become a part of the life of the group.

This has been particularly important in youth cells. We noted at the beginning of the chapter the capacity of young people to live in two worlds at once. Within a group of only fifteen or twenty you can hide when someone preaches, and then you don't have to change. But in a group of four or five it is very difficult to hide. We are encouraged, though, as we see young people start to embrace Christianity with the whole of their lives. As they start to live out their beliefs and values at school with their friends, we have seen very encouraging signs that their evangelism can be highly effective. When we are authentic witnesses, the words we speak resonate.

Mobilisation

Perhaps the most important lesson that we are learning is the need to mobilise the whole of the body of Christ, while recognising just how difficult that actually is. In simple terms, we have had a model in church for 1700 years in which the leaders have been the heroes. We are discovering now that God has a greater dream. God wants his people to be the heroes, and leaders are there to equip those people for the work of ministry.[6] In many ways, this simple vision is the most difficult but the most necessary revolution required in our churches today. If we can mobilise every member of the body of Christ into their God-given ministries and destinies, if we are all salt and light, and if we are all loving our neighbours and reaching out to our world, the church can once again be a huge catalyst for change.

There are a number of challenges involved in doing this. Firstly, many leaders have deeply ingrained ideas about leadership, what it's for and what it should look like. Leaders who want to mobilise the body of Christ need to release people into ministry. It's about letting go rather than holding on tight. In the short term this can be both hard work and risky. But in the long term such an approach is extraordinarily rewarding.

Secondly, in order to nurture an outward focus, to encourage Christians to invest time in their non-Christian friends and contexts, many church structures and meetings need to be pruned. When structures have been embedded in the life of the church over many generations, they can be taken out too quickly, which causes too painful a reaction, or they can be left in place too long, which means people never have time to do anything else. Wisdom is required. Mistakes will be made. The transition to a mobilised church can be messy, and a good deal of explanation and encouragement is required on the way.

Thirdly, mobilisation is hampered through the appallingly low self-image that many British people seem to have. We must continue to disciple people into a biblical view of themselves, so that they can do what God has created them to do.

Fourthly, mobilisation is hampered by a benefit-based culture. In the eighties and nineties people were won into church on a 'be blessed' mandate: 'be healed', 'be whole'. Yet now we are challenging them to *be* a blessing, to work hard, to reach out. We are seeking to create a different culture. If we are honest, within every Christian soul there is a voice that says, 'I would like to be blessed. I'm not sure I want to be a blessing. It's too much. It can't work.' So the cell church has to work against the grain of our benefit-based consumerist society.

Conclusion

In summary, we are grateful for the lessons that we've been learning over the past few years. Indeed we recognise, too, that other streams within the UK church share many of our experiences. We are encouraged that within a cell there can be a great level of accountability, openness and support that encourages discipleship and empowers people to take their faith into every area of their lives. In particular we see that the cell model does create an environment that encourages people to be outward-focused, to love and reach out to the people around them. It also offers support for their call to be salt and light in the workplace. Within cells people begin to see that every-member ministry is the way forward, yet they enjoy the partnership and support that comes from a dynamic small group and from the leadership and times of 'gathering' of the wider church family.

But we also recognise that we face significant challenges from our culture. In order to engage effectively with the world, our discipleship will need to deepen and mature.[7] We must remain open to change, and to changing the ways in which we help Christians to grow as disciples of Christ. This means remaining true to underlying biblical principles, but not being afraid to take on a shape that is dynamic in our culture. We want to be good at John Stott's 'double listening' – listening to the word and to the world.

We have learned that understanding our DNA is crucial to healthy growth and development. We must emphasise the beliefs, the values, the vision and the outcomes on which our movement is based, and be a little more relaxed about the very necessary structures and mechanics that we set in place. We've also learned that we need to intentionally set in place the mechanisms that will protect our DNA and allow us to flourish: mechanisms such as our system of coaches.

We have also recognised that the journey we are on is for the long haul. We need to continue to ask ourselves the questions that help us to get to grips with the underlying barriers to whole-life discipleship, to every-member ministry. We already know much of what we need to be working on, yet we sense there is much more that we will need to wrestle with if we are to really help Christians live fully for Christ in such a radically changing culture.

♦ ♦ ♦ ♦

Notes

1 See chapter 6: Shaping the disciple's mind.

2 For more about the cell movement itself, its origins and models on which it is based try Ralph Neighbour, *Where Do We Go From Here?: A Guidebook for the Cell Group Church* (Touch Publications, 2000), or William Beckham, *The Second Reformation: Reshaping the Church for the Twenty-first Century* (Touch Publications, 1995).

3 Robert Warren, *Building Missionary Congregations* (Church House Publishing, 1996).

4 Mark Greene, *Thank God it's Monday: Ministry in the Workplace* (Scripture Union, 2004).

5 This was a foundational principle of cell pioneer Ralph Neighbour, who was both an evangelist and an educationalist.

6 See chapter 9: What are leaders for?

7 See chapter 6: Shaping the disciple's mind.

16

Experiments in twenty-first-century disciple-making

Jan McCuin

Since coming to faith in Christ in 1967 Jan has been involved with a variety of local churches as she has moved around the country in her career as a speech and language therapist. Jan subsequently joined the staff of The Navigators, working with students in Loughborough, before moving to Newcastle upon Tyne. She is currently part of the team running a pilot scheme that aims to help churches develop a stronger disciple-making culture within their communities.

Many Christians long to make a difference for Christ in their everyday world but aren't sure how to go about it. They don't want more programmes or activities but they do want to engage meaningfully with God in the world and with the people they meet. In this chapter Jan unpacks some early thinking on an innovative new coaching process for church leaders aimed at creating a positive, intentional disciple-making environment in local churches.

For reflection

- What does a twenty-first-century disciple of Christ look like?
- Do you have mechanisms to assess what principles and practices of disciple-making are working in your church?

Experiments in twenty-first-century disciple-making

In 1993 I heard a talk by Adrian Plass on the theme 'Am I the only one?' It's a refrain that I hear echoed amongst many Christians as they reflect about faith and life today. 'Am I the only one who is excited about the something new God is seeking to do, and yet scared sometimes of the changes it may mean, especially in me and for me? I doubt it! Am I the only one who longs for the day when the line between our Sunday faith and the rest-of-our-week life is banished for ever and God is let loose from this place and from our lives to touch a waiting, longing world? I hope not. Am I the only one who sees church as a means and not the end? I doubt it.'

The variety of contributors to this book bears testimony to the fact that many Christians care deeply about the shallowness of our disciple-making in the UK today. And we are not the only ones. Around the country there are hundreds, if not thousands, of thoughtful, prayerful Christians who long to see whole-life disciple-making at the heart of their church life. And there are many, many pastors who desire to help people grow in faith and in mission-hearted Christian living, able to make a difference wherever they are. God's calling to The Navigators as an organisation is 'to advance the Gospel of Jesus and his kingdom into the nations through spiritual generations of labourers living and discipling among the lost'. We have responded to that call in varying ways over the years. In the UK today we are experimenting with a new process of serving the local church called the Intentional Disciple-making Church process (IDC). This has been developed through the American Navigators and we are now adapting this process for the UK, piloting it with a small number of local churches. IDC is clearly one way amongst many to approach this task of helping churches grow as disciple-making communities. But as a contribution to the conversation about how we might broaden and deepen the disciple-making that's happening in the UK church I'd like to outline the IDC process, highlight some of its foundational principles and reflect on what we're learning through our experiments in the UK at the moment.

IDC: what is it?

IDC aims to create a positive, intentional disciple-making culture within local churches, in order to help believers to grow in their faith and become whole-life disciples. These disciples are equipped to pass on what they learn to the next generation of believers. Disciples become disciple-makers. The IDC process is initiated with the leadership team of a local church. It's a consultative relationship between that group and a small team of trained IDC facilitators. The facilitators take the leadership team through a process that lasts around eighteen months. The process comprises four components: mission, spiritual maturity, outreach and leadership. Small groups and 'life to life' are the main ways in which people are helped to grow and so are discussed within each component. Foundational to the process are three dynamics: prayer – focusing on the prayer life of the leaders and corporate prayer for the church's vision and mission; team building – building a team whose members understand each other's gifting, strengths and weaknesses; and assessment – providing feedback on the health and growth of the church.[1]

A number of principles underpin the IDC process. First, it does what it says on the tin – it's a process and not a set programme. Different churches are at different points on the disciple-making journey. They embark on the IDC process by working through the 'foundations'. From that they decide which component they would like to study in depth first. The principle of intentionality is woven into the process throughout. We don't assume that people are learning, or guess how they're getting on. Rather we articulate what and how we want them to learn, and take steps to understand how we're all getting on. The process is designed to give people a biblical understanding of what a disciple looks like and what mature discipleship might look like in a believer's life in this twenty-first century. IDC is about being actively engaged in modelling and mentoring whole-life discipleship – being a disciple-maker. So it helps Christians to move from 'being taught' to engaging in lifelong learning. This is achieved through mutually accountable relationships. IDC is about what happens in the 'gathered' church so that the 'scattered' church is equipped and enabled to live and disciple amongst the lost. Significantly, IDC also focuses on what it means to be a leader of an intentional disciple-making church, paying particular attention to the leader's personal devotional life.

Over the past couple of years I have engaged with a number of local church leaders with IDC on an experimental basis. Those experiments are now developing into a more structured piloting process. We are at the early stages of a long learning curve, but a number of common practical questions and discussion points have arisen from these experiments and I'd like to describe five of these in this chapter.

Why is it so important to stress intentionality in our disciple-making?

The word 'intentional' is one of those words that make people stop and think. It is not used extensively at the moment, yet having lived with it for a couple of years I have seen the term begin to enter everyday language. In the context of a disciple-making church, though, I have found it needs much explanation and discussion. One way that seems to help is to set 'intentional' against 'assumed' when thinking about the nature of disciple-making. When a church assumes that what it does is going to result in healthy, growing disciples rather than approaching disciple-making intentionally and purposefully it usually means that its understanding of disciple-making is fairly broad and unspecific. Often the church's primary vehicle for disciple-making is teaching and preaching. One of the outcomes of this is that the application of the teaching is left almost entirely in the individual's hands. It is assumed everyone will apply and be obedient to the truth they hear. So disciple-making is somewhat haphazard and rather impersonal, and rarely, if ever, goes beyond the next generation. That is, the church rarely sees a consistent pattern emerging of one person helping another who goes on to help the third, and so on.

By contrast, intentional disciple-making focuses on an individual or group of people, so is more targeted. Application of truth is encouraged, as people intentionally hold one another accountable. It is purposeful and planned, and most effective if it happens through close, encouraging relationships. Intentionality is also much more likely to impact a third generation of believers.[2]

There has been some discussion of whether 'intentional' is a British word or not. In the light of our desire to make *whole-life* disciples, an alternative might be 'integrated', by which we mean learning to connect our faith to all areas of our lives. However, this is a different meaning and focus from 'intentional'. Maybe we need both 'intentional and integrated' disciple-making within the local church!

What is the role of the leaders in a disciple-making church?

Two words come to mind: modelling and mentoring. Modelling leads to authenticity. That is, it can do so if leaders model the kind of discipleship that promotes reflection and discussion, vulnerability and self-examination. By trying to live as Christ's disciples in all areas of life, by sharing the struggles and the biblical insights, by discussing and praying with others, leaders both experience and model what it means to be a twenty-first-century disciple of Jesus.

Whilst modelling the life of a disciple, leaders are more able to pass on sound practical help to others. Often this will be through mentoring relationships. A helpful definition of mentoring, that I have worked with for some time, is this. Mentoring is a mutual, biblical relationship – it flows in both directions, although at various times one person may know something while the other is eager to learn. Mentoring has an intentional agenda – there is an agreed end in mind and times to meet will be planned and prepared for. Mentoring is filled with meaningful content – it combines theory and reality, thinking and practice.[3]

If mutual mentoring relationships develop at a leadership level, this models discipling relationships that can be developed more widely within the church membership. If it is effective, these people see the benefits and want to enter into such relationships for themselves. This contributes to the development of a positive environment for disciple-making throughout the church family: for example, discussions over coffee may naturally turn to how people have been affected by the truth they've heard rather than yesterday's football results. Then, if they are experiencing such conversations within the 'safe' confines of church, perhaps they will begin to transfer these to their everyday lives.

What benefits have emerged from assessment procedures that IDC encourages?

Every church is at a different stage of putting into practice the Great Commission. So, for example, one church held Matthew 28:18-20 highly. The pastor made sure he met with one individual from the congregation on a regular weekly basis for a year, in order to help them grow. The pastor also encouraged each person on the diaconate to 'train up their replacement' by meeting with them regularly, again for the period of a year. They had an extensive system of small groups. Yet when we started talking about intentionally making disciples it was clear that he thought mainly in terms of programmes. This meant our conversation quickly veered into what group of people could be put through which programme rather than thinking how a positive disciple-making culture could become the culture of the whole church.

Another church saw preaching, teaching and their small group structure as the main means of helping people grow as disciples. No personal help was offered, and the small group system was mainly for the fellowship of those who had been church members and

Christians a long time. New believers, with no church background, found both the large group and small group settings totally alien. Yet another church had a growing desire to see the Great Commission being worked out among their people, but admitted they didn't know where to start.

Assessing where any given church is on the spectrum of putting the Great Commission into practice is a good starting point. It is not a question of the church thinking they have to abandon what they are currently doing. Rather it is helpful to assess what disciple-making principles and practices are currently in place and then, through study, discussion and example, introduce into the church a positive disciple-making culture that encourages all believers to become whole-life disciples.

What part does 'Life to Life' play in disciple-making?

In Matthew 28:18-20, having stated that all authority in heaven and earth has been given to him, Jesus goes on to say, 'Go therefore and make disciples of all nations, baptising them . . . and teaching them to obey everything I have commanded . . . and remember, I am with you always, to the end of the age.' Other versions translate the opening statement 'therefore as you go' (ISV), or 'disciple all the nations' (YLT). So what was Jesus saying here? As part of going about your everyday business, disciple others: get involved with them and enable them to meet Jesus and grow to know him more deeply; encourage them to live a life of obedience to him.

To help us understand what this means, let's look at the term 'Life to Life', an expression defined by Bennett and Purvis as 'Two or more people in an intentional, purposeful, learning experience where each is committed to Christian discipleship, transparency and full maturity. The relational dynamic between (these) people enables the transfer of knowledge, heart, vision and skill for becoming mature and wholehearted followers of Christ.'[4] 'Life to Life' is where two people have a rich relationship and intentionally seek to learn from one another. Growing in life, in faith and in mission is a complex process. Many different kinds of relationship have a part to play in this: the relationships within the whole church, those that operate in a small group setting, and one-to-one interpersonal relationships.

How can the 'gathered' church help its people to be whole-life disciples when they are the 'scattered' church?

This is a challenge. How can we enable and encourage people to live as Christ's disciples seven days a week and not simply view the times when we meet together as the whole church family as the most important times in a disciple's life? Jim Peterson and Mike Shamy describe the life of a man, Jack, in their book *The Insider*.[5] Jack is at the top of his profession, and has a good marriage and family. He has been a Christian for as long as he can remember. Yet one day he says, 'These past twenty years of my life have played out like a bad movie. As I watched them go by I kept thinking to myself, "This wasn't the script I had in mind. It wasn't supposed to be like this . . . and I don't know what I can do to make the next twenty any different."' Jack is not alone. Many Christians today in our churches are looking to make an impact for Christ in their everyday world but aren't sure how to go about it. They don't want more programmes or activities but they do want to engage with God's purposes in the world amongst the people where God has placed them. So these are the challenges to which we want to rise with the IDC process. To avoid falling into the programmatic trap. To help strengthen churches to resist the forces that pull them inwards and to help them look outwards. To keep the end goal in mind – to equip Christians to live full, integrated, Gospel-infused lives wherever God places them and whatever the challenges this brings.

For our churches to become whole-life disciple-making communities we will need faith and a lot of hard work. But it seems to me that the Lord is opening up some hugely exciting and imaginative possibilities for different organisations and streams within the UK church to share resources and engage together around this common vision. We have much to learn through all such experiments, including the IDC process. I trust that over time the IDC process will contribute meaningfully to this goal of churches becoming whole-life disciple-making communities.

♦ ♦ ♦ ♦

Further reading and resources

Bennett, Ron, *Intentional Disciplemaking: Cultivating Spiritual Maturity in the Local Church* (Navpress, 2001)

For more information about the *Intentional Disciple-making Church Process* contact The Navigators, Turner House, 54 The Avenue, Southampton, SO17 1XQ. Tel: 023 8055 8800. Email: info@navigators.co.uk Website: www.navigators.co.uk

Notes

1 For more detail visit www.navigators.org/us/ministries/cdm/idc

2 As per Paul in 2 Tim. 2:2: 'What you have heard from me through many witnesses entrust to faithful people who will be able to teach others as well.'

3 Taken from the Navigator 2:7 discipleship programme.

4 Ron Bennett and John Purvis, *The Adventure of Discipling Others: Training in the Art of Disciplemaking* (Navpress, 2003).

5 Jim Petersen and Mike Shamy, *The Insider: Bringing the Kingdom of God into your Everyday World* (Navpress, 2003).

Postscript: creating disciple-making churches today

Postscript

The Imagine Project

Tracy Cotterell

It's one thing to reflect on and wrestle with the issues we face in helping Christians grow so that they can make a greater impact in today's world. It's an altogether different challenge to know how to move forward practically with the people we know and in the church contexts we lead or inhabit.

This collection of reflections on disciple-making originated at an LICC conference in March 2005, where several of these chapters were presented, though in a slightly different format. The conference and this collection are some of the fruit from LICC's *Imagine Project*, a widely supported initiative to revitalise whole-life Christian disciple-making in the UK today. *Imagine* is intended as a catalyst serving the wider UK church as we learn to create and sustain whole-life disciple-making communities that help people grow in faith and in their ability to align all of their lives with God's story and his mission in this world.

In our contemporary culture this is a major challenge. It's a challenge because maturity is itself an elusive quality. And it's a challenge because most people agree that there is no one model for disciple-making, nor indeed is the 'solution' to be found by alighting on or creating another programme or methodology.

For many churches, becoming a whole-life disciple-making community will involve a major shift in their culture. So the *Imagine Project* is focused in three areas:

1. Vision

We need to really grasp the significance of 'whole-life disciple-making' for mission in the UK and to imagine what such communities might look like in today's world. In the spirit of Hebrews 10:24, *Imagine* is designed to incite, provoke and encourage one another to wholeheartedly embrace this challenge.

2. Research and development

Through a combination of biblical, theological and practical research with a small number of 'pilot' local churches *Imagine* will, in the medium term, serve the wider UK church with biblically astute and practically robust wisdom, to help leaders and their communities move forward in their own contexts. The three-year experimental local church pilot programme starts in autumn 2006.

3. Training

The training of church leaders, both those in pastoral ministry and the wider leadership within churches, is clearly a key dynamic for change. A primary outcome of the project will be focused and flexible training modules that churches and other organisations will be able to access and integrate into their own approaches to training leaders.

This task of developing whole-life disciple-making communities is self-evidently beyond the remit of any one part of the body of Christ. So LICC is committed to working in partnership with denominations and other organisations that are gripped by this need and that are developing initiatives and resources that connect into this vision for discipleship today.

The *Imagine Project* has four published resources available to date:

Imagine how we can reach the UK *(£3.50, book, 2004, ISBN 1-85078-544-9 available from your Christian bookshop or www.authenticmedia.co.uk)*
Intended as a catalyst for debate about reaching the UK in today's new culture, this essay develops a diagnosis of the state of the nation and of the church. Its conclusion is simple: the recovery of whole-life disciple-making is the key to reaching our nation today.

Imagine: Let My People Grow *(£3, magazine, 2005)*
Published in partnership with the Evangelical Alliance, this magazine follows on from the first essay, unpacking two core values that can help church communities grow whole-life apprentices who will together reach out to our hurting, needy nation.

Imagine how we can reach the UK *(£10, DVD, 2006)*
Designed as a resource for large or small groups in one, two or three sessions, the DVD consists of the main fifty-minute film, plus exercises, questionnaires, a discussion guide, supplementary interviews with leaders and a PowerPoint presentation. Based around the first essay and follow up magazine, the film explores the main reasons for the church's difficulties in envisioning, equipping, resourcing and supporting Christians for today's world and proposes a simple but radical way forward, focusing on two great biblical truths – the concern of the Creator-redeemer God for every aspect of our lives and Jesus' mandate to make disciples, not converts.

Let My People Grow *(£17, eight-disc audio CD pack, 2005)*
This is a collection of recordings from the March 2005

LICC Imagine Conference, which catalysed this book collection. The set contains seven plenary talks and two seminars from some of the authors contributing to this book. This CD set is helpful for those who prefer to access material in audio format or for use on the move.

For more details on these resources or to obtain copies call LICC on 020 7399 9555 or visit www.licc.org.uk/bookshop.

LICC also runs a series of *Imagine* workshops for church leaders throughout the year in partnership with RUN (Reaching the Unchurched Network). A further set of workshop materials for use with local church congregations has been tested and is being developed for wider use.

For more about the *Imagine Project*, including details of the workshops, new resources and the three-year experimental local church pilot programme visit www.licc.org.uk/imagine.

Tracy Cotterell
Director, *Imagine Project*
LICC
St Peter's
Vere Street
London W1G 0DQ
(t) 020 7399 9555
(e) mail@licc.org.uk
(w) www.licc.org.uk